# Family Business:
## The Gift-The Curse

To my brother
Warren. Amazing trainer
& even better person
Thanks for your support

Benny

### By
### Ben Thornton

# Contents

# Chapter 1

# **The Early Years**

My pops always told me that I would go to jail if I took this life. I knew one day it would happen. I just didn't know when. My parents were like most. They just wanted a better life for their kids. My pops was 49 and my mom was 29 when I was born on February 17, 1972. Yes, you heard right 20 years apart. Pops always considered himself a player. He was very fair skinned, with silky black hair. Born Benjamin Thomas Thornton in 1923 in Washington D.C., he was the middle of 13 kids. He was an altar boy as a child. His mom died when he was around 9 years old. His father later died when he was around 20. He then took on the responsibility of taking care of his younger siblings in the house they had grown up in on Defrees Street which no longer exists. He took care of his younger siblings as long as he could. In his teen years he had learned how to cheat at gambling with dice. He would win money and that's how he supported himself and siblings. One day before his dad had passed, he won a large sum of money and offered it to his dad to help with the family's bills. His dad turned down the money and told him he would not accept any illegal money.

My pops dropped out of school around the 10<sup>th</sup> grade. His dad told him he had three choices, either you go to school, work or leave the house. He got some odd jobs. In his early twenties he decided to join the army. The skill he had learned of cheating at dice came in handy, because the guys in the army loved to gamble. After a while he no longer wanted to be in the army and went AWOL. He told me his entire platoon got killed. I guess if he didn't go AWOL I wouldn't be here today writing this story. He went back to his old ways of gambling, but now he was also introduced to the drug trade. He began selling pills and later on moved on to selling heroin. He had fathered six daughters. One by a woman whom I never met. Her daughter was named Pauline and she was the oldest of all the girls. I probably remember seeing her a total of 5 times in my life. He had three more daughters with Riley, whom he would later marry. My sisters Benita, Shelly and Bianca were all definitely in my life growing up. He would also father 2 more girls by two different women. My sisters Dina and Bonnie. I guess you can say my pops was a rolling stone. One thing I will say about him is he always took care of all of his kids. My mom was born in 1942 in Statesville, N.C. Barbara Jean McNeely. She never talked about her parents, but I always felt like it was some sort of trauma. She was raised by her aunt Laura (Snook). She came to Washington, D.C., when she was teenager. She dropped out of school in the ninth grade to work and take care of herself. My mom would go on to have two children of her own. My brother Eddie Murphy, no not that Eddie Murphy, who we called Darrell and my sister Ann. She actually married my sister Ann's father and became Barbara Cook. Around 1969 my parents met at a party. I remember my mom telling me her girlfriend was interested in my pops. As I stated he was a handsome man. Very fair skin, with silky hair and grey eyes. She said in her mind that she was going to get him, and she did. My mom was always a petite woman, with shapely legs. They began dating and she became pregnant. She got an abortion and almost died during the procedure. She got pregnant again and this time she was not going to go through that. They decided to keep the baby. My mom, pops, Darrell and Ann lived in an apartment in S.E. Washington D.C. Once my mom decided to keep the baby, she told my dad that she wanted to live in a house. In December of 1971 they brought a beautiful single-family home, with five bedrooms, 3 baths, 3 fireplaces, and 2 full kitchens in the suburbs of Maryland.

I was born February 17, 1972, in S.E. Memorial hospital Benjamin Thomas Thornton. My dad never used senior and I never used junior and this would come into play later in my life. My early childhood years where great. I was the baby boy that my pops always wanted. You can imagine as the baby boy I was spoiled rotten. Some of my oldest memories are of me getting into trouble for playing in the toilet and my dad spanking me with a belt. I had little welts on my leg and my pops freaked out and wanted to take me to the hospital. My mom laughed and told him they would be gone by the morning and they were. I just remember always being showered with gifts and toys. In 1977 a traumatic incident happened, and I really didn't know what was going on. These men broke into our house with guns and were screaming and yelling at my parents. They had pointed a shotgun at my sister and mom went crazy and started yelling and cursing at them. At the time I didn't know it, but these men were federal agents and were serving a warrant to search our home. My dad was a numbers bookie. A numbers bookie was a person who did what our government now today does called the lottery. You would play your numbers with one of my pops runners and they would turn that number into my pops. If your number came out my pops would then pay you. I assume it was illegal because the government was not getting any taxes off of the proceeds. They took my pops to jail, but I was told he went into the army. We would go visit him in Lorton Penitentiary, in Lorton V.A. I remember writing him a letter one night while sitting on my mom's lap. I fell asleep while writing the letter and mom finished it for me. He was later moved to Lewisburg Federal penitentiary in Lewisburg P.A. We would only get to see him on Sundays. I remember on one trip I was going to visit him with my sisters, Shelly, Bianca and Benita. My nephew LB shouted out were going to see granddaddy in jail. I screamed jail. My sisters quickly tried to correct him and tell him to shut up. LB was 2 years older than me and named after my pops. I assume they thought he was not going to have any boys. He would take his dads last name of though. My pops was locked up in the feds for 3 years on this particular charge. It was not the first time he had been incarcerated, and it wouldn't be his last. Although he was incarcerated nothing in the household changed financially. I still got everything a kid could want. Always the newest and freshest clothes. As I got a little older. I knew he was no longer in the army. I remember kids would ask me where my father was. I would just say he was away.

In 1978 I started to play little league football for the Silver Hill boys and girls club. My first year I started out playing right guard. One time the running back rammed his head into my back, and I knew I didn't want to play guard anymore. The next season I went out for running back and soon became the star of the team. My parents always told me one thing. You can play football as long as you make good grades. I generally made the honor roll all the way through my school years. The year of 1980 was an amazing year for me, and my life took on a new twist.  My pops was released from prison and I was so happy for him to be home.  We would get up in the morning before school and we would jog around the block.  I remember him buying us five new sweat suits a piece that matched. I asked him why he bought us five? He said we had to wear a different one every day.  My pops and mom were always sharp dressers. They made sure me, Ann, and Darrell had the best of the best.  My pops took care of Ann and Darrell as if they were his own kids. We all used to get an allowance and I would get mad because they got more than me. I was like, why does he give them more than me when he's my pops. Truth be told Darrell was ten years older than me and Ann was 8.  Growing up me and Darrell were not extremely close. Not sure if it was the age difference or him constantly being gone and getting into trouble.  I remember when I was about 3 years old my cousin David left us in the car with car running. He ran into the store and Darrell got behind the wheel and started driving the car. We were parked next to a car dealership, and he hit several new cars.  I slammed my face against the dashboard busting my lip and my parents had to pay for the damage to the cars he had hit.  He was good in academics as well as sports. He had trophies for football, boxing and even golf, but he just always thought he was smarter than everyone else.

Me and my sister Ann had the love hate relationship that siblings have growing up. She hated to have her little brother tag along, but you better not mess with her little brother.  I remember this little white kid called me a nigger. I didn't know what the word meant at the time. I asked Ann, what did the word mean.  She asked me why? I told her the little white kid had called me a nigger. I didn't know what it meant, but I knew it was not good because she immediately went over to the boy and started pounding on him. She followed him all the way home beating him up. The whole neighborhood was out playing, and we all followed her as well.  When we got to his house his dad came out and told my sister to go home before he wraps her bike around her neck. She told him if he touches her momma will come around here and wrap the bike around his ass.  We all laughed but we all wind up leaving.  My sister was hot headed and never scared to fight anyone.  She used to whip my butt constantly.  She said to make me tougher, because I was a little punk.

4

Well maybe not a punk, but I was always the smallest and youngest of most of my friends. I remember one time one of my friends Tone hit me in my back and I began to cry. I told him I was going to get my sister. He ran to his brother Vince and said lock all the doors and windows Ann is coming to get me. I went and got Ann and we rang his doorbell. She told him to come outside. She ordered me to hit him and told him he better not hit me back, so I did, and he didn't touch me.

Growing up in my house definitely had its pros and cons, but now that my pops was back home it seemed only pros. I told my pops I wanted a motorized dirt bike. I remember my pops would wake me up in the middle of the night to help him count money. I never understood why he would have me count the money and then he would count it behind me. I counted thousands and thousands of dollars. One particular night he told me to count a stack of money. It was $800 dollars. He looked at me and said that's the money for your dirt bike. I smiled from ear to ear. The next day we went to the Honda dealership and I picked out a red Honda 50. I went home and told all my friends my pops had brought me a dirt bike and it would be delivered tomorrow. All my friends had talked about getting a dirt bike, but none of their parents had brought them one. I remember all of us getting off the school bus the next day and running to my house. We ran down into the basement, but there was no dirt bike. The next day we did the exact same thing and still no dirt bike. I started to question if my pops had really bought it. The third day I was like it's probably not here. When we opened up the basement door and that new shiny red Honda 50 was sitting there, my face lit up with joy. Now the problem was that no one knew how to even get it started. All my friends had claimed they had ridden before. We had to call my sister's friend George to come and start it. The problem was it was in gear. He quickly showed me how to ride and we all were flying around my back yard destroying the grass. My mom came home and cussed all of us out and told us to take the bike onto the street. At the time we didn't know it was illegal to ride on the street. Tone was the first to crash on my bike and I told him he couldn't ride anymore. I remember that this girl I really liked named Mona wanted me to ride her around on my bike, so I did. One day while I was riding her around the neighborhood. This white man

5

in a white plain car pulled up beside me and told me to pull over. I was about 4 houses away from mine and told him I was going to get my mom. He grabbed me by the neck. My sister and brother happened to be outside and saw him grabbing me. My sister immediately ran down and punched him in his face. I proceeded to bite him, and he released me and grabbed my sister. My brother ran pass me and he also punched the guy in the face. He released my sister and ran to his car and called for backup. I ran into the house and screamed for my mom. My sister and brother followed me into the house. Before we knew it there were at least 5 police cars on our street. They wanted to press charges against my brother and sister and my mom stated she would also press charges against the officer because I had marks around my neck from where he had grabbed me. In the end no charges were filed, but they did impound my dirt bike. My pops came home and went to pay to get my bike out of the impound. After that my mom told me not to ride the bike unless her or my pops were home. A couple months later someone broke into our shed and stole my bike. A week later my pops bought me a bigger and better bike, a Suzuki DS 80. This one had a clutch and gear shifter like real motorcycles and even had a headlight and brake light. He told me if this one gets stolen that he would not buy me another one, so I better make sure the shed was secure.

Life was going wonderful. I remember my pops coming to my little league football games. He would give me $100 dollars for every touchdown I scored. I didn't usually score more than 2, but usually always scored at least 1. The players on my team found out and ragged on me saying they should get a share. On Sundays they would allow me to pick out a restaurant from this restaurant book my mom had purchased. We would all get dressed up and go to dinner. Me and my dad would wear suits. One time when we went to dinner and the hostess said let me take your coats. I started to take mine off and my pops popped me in the back of the head and told me to leave my coat on. He said he's talking to the women. Men keep their coats on during dinner. One Sunday my pops was upset with me and he didn't take us to dinner with him. He was upset with me because earlier that day he had given me $10,000 dollars to hide. I had a whole set of new encyclopedias in my room on my bookshelf. I decided to hide the money in the encyclopedias. The problem was it would not fit into one, so I had to divide it amongst them. He came in later and asked me what I did with the money. When I told him he was surprised, and he looked pleased that I had found a good hiding place. He asked me which one and that's when his pleasure turned to anger because I didn't remember which one. We were shaking the books trying to find the money because they were brand new and had never really been used, so the pages were sticking. He began to yell at me, and my mom yelled at him for giving me the money. He said he was teaching me some sort of responsibility. I was about 10. We found the money and they went off to dinner just the two of them. My pops was usually nice and pleasant. I can only remember one time in my life he actually told me no to something I asked him for. He just had a deep voice that even when he said yes, it terrified me as a kid. That night at dinner he called home. When my sister told me he was on the phone, I began to cry. I got to the phone and he apologized for screaming at me and said he was sorry, I was still crying and said ok. That night while he was out at dinner his pager went off. Back in those days only 2 people really had pagers. Doctors and drug dealers. A white gentleman tapped my father on the shoulder and said, "excuse me doctor your pager is going off." My pops looked at him, laughed and replied, "the hospital can't make it without me some nights." As I stated life was full of pros and not just for me. My mom was showered with all types of gifts from diamonds, mink coats, shopping sprees and trips. She would get a new Cadillac every year, until 1983 when she got a new 1984 Mercedes Benz. My mom was funny because she loved the Cadillac Seville until they changed the shape. She said she would never get another one. Until my pops talked her into getting a new car. She also said she would never get a Mercedes, because the diesel engines at the time sounded like a Mack truck. The next thing I knew she was driving a new Mercedes. When Ann turned 16 he bought her a car as well.

I remember one day he took me shopping and I was looking at some pants. I walked away from the pants once I saw the price. My pops asked me what's wrong and I told him they cost too much. He asked me, why was I worried about what they cost, I was not paying for them and if I

7

wanted them to get them.  I got them and soon learned the difference about having money. That was just the life he gave to all of us. If he had it and you wanted it or needed, then he made sure you got it. In 1984 life seemed like it could get no better.  Little did I know my dad had once again been arrested for possession with the intent to distribute heroin.

# Chapter 2

# The Day My Life Changed

On February 17, 1984, my twelfth birthday, my parents informed me that my pops had court that day and I would be going to court instead of school. I really didn't understand or know what to expect. He had hired some high price lawyer whom advised him against me going into the courtroom. He said it would seem like we were trying to get sympathy from the Jury. I was not allowed into the court room and my pops was found guilty. I was hurt and angry all at the same time. I could not believe this had just happened. He was sentenced to 15 years and 1 special under the old federal law, before they changed it to mandatory 85%. Later that day my mom took me out for dinner at one of my favorite restaurants which was the Golden Bull, but as you can imagine I had no appetite. I was scared, angry and nervous. She consoled me and told me everything would be ok. The next day she told me to get the ladder out of the shed. I had no idea why, but I knew my dad would get the ladder out of the shed some nights. She placed the ladder under one of the openings in the ceiling and climbed up pushed it open and went up into the attic. She later came down with a metal box. She used a key to open it and it was full of money. She told me to help her count it. It was almost $150,000 dollars in this box. I guess financially we would be ok. My pops was sent to a federal penitentiary in Springfield, Missouri, and I didn't get the opportunity to see him until that summer when we got out for summer break. Me, my mom and my uncle Jimmy went up for 3 weeks. I remember being excited to see my pops. He called home often, so we talked all the time, but I missed seeing him. I remember being so happy at him picking me up and hugging. My mom was not a happy camper though. She found out some other woman had visited my pops and was not happy about that. For the next 3 weeks we stayed in a hotel. Springfield was different. Not many Black people. The whole time I was there I only remember seeing 2 other Black people outside of the penitentiary. One day I was in the pool with these 2 white girls. Their dad was talking to my uncle. I guess my uncle was bragging on me because I was good with computers and was on the honor roll. I remember the dad saying to his daughters that I would make a good catch. At the time I had no idea what he was talking about. One day when me and my uncle were walking into the mall this white guy looked at us and said "wow nice to see you." I said hello and looked my uncle. He laughed and said they don't see many Black people here. I have to admit although there were basically no Black people I never felt out of place or uncomfortable. At the end of the three weeks I didn't want to go, but I knew the time had come. My pops and mom seem to have made up. We left and I just wished my pops was leaving with us. When I got back home. I was in the local drug store Dart Drug. I was looking in the candy aisle and I saw that you could get 10 packs of gum for $1.25. I said to myself I bet I could sell those for 25 cents per pack. So, I brought them and took them to school the next day and sold all of them. Doubling my profit. I went back to the drugstore the next day and brought other candy and took them to school and also sold them for a profit. Everything was going smooth until one of my classmates, a white girl named Dawn, asked me for some candy. I asked if she had any money and she said no. I told her no money, no candy. She told our teacher I was selling candy, and on my way out at the end of the day he grabbed my bag and looked in it. They called my mom and she had to come up to the school. They said since I was a good student and had never been in any trouble, they would not suspend me as long as I promised not to do it again. I didn't understand the big deal, but my mom looked at me and said, "tell them you promise." One thing I do know you don't argue with Barbara Jean. I agreed and it never happened again. She asked me on the ride home why did I do it? She said it's not like you need the money and she was right. If I wanted money for something all I had to do was ask. I guess somehow just like my pops I always had the hustle inside me. I was a little scared on the way home because my mom although a petite woman swung a mean belt. She was always the primary disciplinarian even when my pops was around. She told me I was not in trouble just don't do it again. It almost took me back to the one time I stole in my life. I was at the candy store and I had money, but the guy left out and I stole some candy. I was with one of my friends who lived across the street and he told my mom. She gave me one of the worse butt whippings I had ever had. That was the last time I stole something. I think I was about 11. It was the mid 80's and the drugs in the DC area were booming.

All the hustlers had the fly cars, money, jewels and girls. My sister use to date some hustlers and they would come over in their cars and I remember being like dam, I want that. With my pops I never really knew that he was a hustler. He didn't drive a fancy car or have a bunch of jewelry and of course I never seen any women except for my mom. He did have some fly clothes. He always had a really nice watch and he wore one big diamond ring on his pinky. He was what you would look at as a classy dresser. Never any jeans, always slacks or s suit. I knew nothing about the drug trade, but I knew I wanted all this stuff I saw these dudes having. At this age you never think about the consequences of, death, jail or destruction. Two years into my pops sentence they moved him back to Lewisburg penitentiary. He was on the camp this time and not behind the wall. I was joking with my mom on going to see him behind the wall. When you go behind the wall you have to go through a metal gate and then wait for that gate to close and another metal gate to open. While waiting for the gate to close a possum ran in and my mom freaked the fuck out. She started screaming open this dame gate. I had no idea what the possum was at the time, so I guess I really wasn't scared. The camp was less security. It actually had no fence or bars at all. You could walk away if you wanted too. My pops explained that some guys would sneak out at night and meet women at the hotel down the street. He explained how stupid it was because if you got caught you got an automatic 5 years and sent behind the wall. I remember going to see him and asking, "why do they make you pull out your pockets?" He looked at my mom, and she looked back and said tell him. He said some guys cut out their pockets out so their women can play with them. I was still not understanding at the time. Before you get to thinking I'm a moron, I was already sexually active at this point. I was molested when I was 6 by a female cousin. She took me out to the shed in our back yard and made me get on top of her. I never really told anyone until I was an adult. Also growing up the neighbors across the street owned a video store. We would get videos from them. One day she handed me some videos, and some were in a paper bag. She instructed me not to look at the videos in the paper bag. I definitely didn't look at them. Not until I got in my house and closed the door. I remember the video was Debbie Does Dallas and some other titles I don't remember. I called up my friends and told them we were going to watch them when my parents were not home. One day when everyone was gone. We watched them. I remember getting aroused. I was about 11 at the time. I also remember the guy shooting cum all over the women and saying ugh, I hope that stuff never comes out of my dick. Little did I know about real sex and the pleasures that came along with ejaculation. We would go see my pops every Sunday and I would tell him about my week. I remember one day getting off of the school bus and a police officer pulled up to us and asked if anyone knew where a Chinese family lived. I told them yes, they live on my street. He put me in the car and told me to slouch down in the seat and point when we pass the house. He took me down the street and let me sit in the driver's seat of the police car and took my picture. I was happy and all my friends thought it was cool. I was waiting to see my pops that Sunday so I could tell him. When I got there and told him the story, he had a mean scowl on his face and ordered me to follow him outside. Once we got outside, he explained to me that what I had done was called a snitch and that men don't snitch or respect snitches. He told me to always mind my own business and never get into anyone else's business. He said that family could come back and kill me or my mother, because we didn't know what they were into or what was going on. That didn't go the way I expected, but I had a new and full understanding of minding my own business. On the way home my mom confirmed what my dad had said. My mom was a petite woman but one of the strongest women I have ever known. I remember one day I was at the basketball court and this older guy about 30 years old asked me for the ball. I was dribbling the ball and I told him no. He came over and started beating me up. He told me when I ask you for the ball you give it to me. I was bent over crying. As I started to walk away. He said go get your mother and father and I'll do the same to them. I definitely couldn't tell my father because he was in the feds. I guess I'll have to chalk up this ass whooping. When I got home, I had tears running down my face and I was holding my side. My mom asked what happened and I told her nothing. She asked me again in a voice that meant nothing was not going to be accepted. I told her this man hit me. She asked me how old and when I told her she went into her room. She only had a house coat on at first, but she returned with a coat and told me to come on. I yelled no we can't go back he said he would hit you too. She said don't worry he won't hit me. I remember driving back around to the court in pure fear. What was I going to do to protect my mom? We pulled up and got out she said point him out. I reluctantly did. All of a sudden, my mom pulls out a 38 snub nose and points at the guy. She said are you the mother fucker that hit my son. He said I was just playing. She told him he's too old and big to playing with kids my age. I said he said he was going to hit you too Ma. She said oh you are going to hit me. Once again, he's shaking and saying I'm sorry I was just playing. She told him if he ever does anything to me that she would kill him. I never had any more trouble out of that dude. On the way home I asked her had she ever shot anyone. She told me no, but she had shot at them. She told me about a time that these men were harassing her and her girlfriends in a new car my father had just got. I believe he kicked the car and she shot a couple holes in his car before he jumped in and sped off. Another time she was actually arrested for shooting at one of my sister's aunts. My sister's aunt slapped my mom and mom shot at her. She said she thought she hit her because she fell. I guess she fell in fear. My pops got my mom a lawyer and the case was settled. My mom was my best friend; growing up made me a strong man along with my pops. She showed me how to be compassionate, humble, but most of all don't take no shit off anyone.

A couple weeks later me and a friend Craig had an idea that we were going to sell weed. He said his dad used to grow it. We went into these Jamaicans yard and he pulled up some weed plants. We replanted them. The operation was called the elephant. We would use the code name elephant whenever talking about weed. Of course, he had no idea what the fuck he was doing the weed never grew. Craig was a little crazy to me. We got into an argument with a lady in the drive thru window about his change being incorrect and he was going to shoot her with his pellet gun. I grabbed the gun and the lady screams oh my God he has a gun. We pulled off laughing. No police were called, because that could have turned out very different. My second stint at getting into the drug game was with one of my best friends Miguel. We were in the 8<sup>th</sup> grade. We decided to buy some cocaine from this guy Martin. We gave him $300 dollars total and he gave us something that was not cocaine. I had one of my older friends who said he knew about cocaine named Russell come over. He did a line and told me that it was definitely not cocaine. Miguel wanted to beat the guy up. I took it as a lesson not to buy something from people you can't trust. I put the dope game on the back burner and wanted to concentrate on football. I was about to go to high school and wanted to go to a school with a good football program. I was always one of the star running backs on my little league football team. I also used to play linebacker or cornerback.

I watched the papers to see the rankings at the beginning and the end of the year. There was a school in Virginia, T.C. Williams and a school in D.C., Archbishop Carroll. In the end Carroll was ranked number 1 and won the championship in their division. I told my pops I wanted to attend Carroll to play football. He told my Uncle jimmy to help me with the procedure and he would pay for it no matter the cost. I filled out the paperwork and I was required to take a test. I remember being so nervous, because I thought this test was the determining factor on whether I got in or not. The test was actually a placement test. I remember the cost being somewhere around $2,500, and an extra couple hundred if you were not Catholic, which I wasn't. My pops was a Catholic, but that didn't count for me. I was told I was accepted. I doubt if they turned anyone down that could pay. I remember getting my class schedule and in front of all my classes it had HON. I had no idea what that meant, so I called my uncle Jimmy. He informed me that meant I would be taking all honors classes. I told him no way. I didn't want to do that. See in my public school I always did good and made the honor roll, but we also had what they called TAG, which stood for talented and gifted and I never wanted to be in that class either. In elementary based on my test scores they consulted my mom and wanted to put me a grade ahead twice to which she declined. I asked her why and she told me she wanted me to develop with people my own age. I was already one of the smaller kids. So here we go to Carroll. I remember being a little intimidated with the honors classes in the beginning. I'm definitely a clever individual. The difference to me between a smart individual and a clever individual is this, a smart person looks at the question and knows the answer, where a clever individual looks at the question and although he may not know it, he can figure it out. That's why I have always been a good test taker because I was clever.

# Chapter 3

# **High School Years**

The first day of school I felt like I was in class with the revenge of the nerds. These guys were super smart, but at the same time definitely nerds. I knew a few guys in my class that played football because practice had started before school. Our class was 1A and it went all the down I believe to 1D. I don't think it meant you were not smart if you were in 1D, just maybe you didn't take test well. The other classes definitely picked on people in our class. During football Season I became good friends with a guy named Turk. He was also in all honors like me. We had also played against each other during little league football. We became best friends. Another guy in our class name Erol was also cool with us. We formed a group called BET which stood for Benny, Erol, and Turk. We would make sure the other guys wouldn't come in our room and pound on our classmates. It was all in good fun, but we were I guess somewhat the defenders of the nerds. Later another classmate whom also played football said something to us for some reason and we jumped on him. Once again it was guys just playing. I remember him getting a knot on his head and we said we wanted to write BET on it jokingly. He later joined us, and we were BETT, because his name was Terry. That school year did not go well. I was not getting any playing time on the field in football. It wasn't that I wasn't good enough, but there was some favoritism going on because some dads knew the coach. After 7 games of not getting any game time on the field. I decided to quit. I didn't tell my parents. I went to the coach and told him that my parents had instructed me to quit because my grades were slipping. I remember him getting upset and yelling and telling me that we don't practice on Fridays so how am I not keeping up with my grades. I wanted to ask him why are you mad? You don't even play me. I then told my parents I was not doing well in school academically and I wanted to transfer to Crossland close to home. My mom came to my school and talked with our dean of men and my teachers. All of my teachers told her I was doing well and had at least a

B or better average in all of my classes. My parents knew I was not getting any playing time and knew that probably was the reason I wanted to transfer. They told me no. I had to continue going to Carroll whether I played football or not. My pops always stressed to me how important an education was. He told me I was smarter than him, and I have a lot more opportunities than he did being born in 1923. That summer was a tough summer. I had a lot of confusion. I told them the only way I would return to Carroll is if I got a car when I got my driver's license. They agreed as long as I kept my grades up. I took a driving class and got my learners permit. Me and my mom told him I could drive with my learners permit so he authorized for my mom to buy me a car. I wanted a Volkswagen Jetta, but my mom bought me a Chevy Nova. I was pissed, when most kids would be grateful to get anything. I felt like you drive a Benz, my sister Has a nice Maxima and you get me a Chevy. None of my friends had cars mostly because none had a license, but neither did I. I had a car and still was not satisfied. I hated driving that car and didn't take care of it at all. I rarely checked, changed the oil or anything, just put gas in it. If one of my older friends that did have a license would want to drive, I would just get in the back. It did however start me to get a lot of attention from high school girls which was kind of a plus. Let me say this though, I always got attention from females. When I was in junior high school. I was voted most popular, best dressed and most likely to succeed. The succeed part had to do with me being popular. I was always known as the kid with the parents with money.

When my pops went to jail my mom started a clothing and jewelry business. I had access to a lot of jewelry, and I would sneak and wear it to school. I remember one incident at a local skating rink when I was in the 9th grade. I had worn some very expensive jewelry that my mom had no idea I had on. This guy I knew pulled a gun on me and told me to give it to him. I told him, you know who my father is and if something happens to me, he is going to have you killed. To be honest I just made that up. I don't know if he knew who my father was. I do know I would have been scared to death to go home and face my mom without that jewelry. He laughed and said he was just playing and walked away. I guess that was the first time somebody wanted to rob me, but definitely wouldn't be the last. That next week in school was some new shit with Tuck. See Tuck was the class clown and was always making fun of people. Some people would get sensitive when he made jokes about them. There was one guy that Tuck would call Hungry, Hungry Hank. Maybe his name was Hank. Hank was a linebacker on the Varsity football team. Big dude you really didn't want to mess with. He was play boxing with another kid and he wind up splitting the dudes head open. He told Turk and us to stop calling him that. One day as we were driving away from the school. Tuck decided to call him Hungry, Hungry Hank. This dude proceeds to chase my car and I kept driving. He screams out "Benny I'm going to fuck you up tomorrow." Everyone in the car was laughing. I didn't think a dam thing was funny. After I dropped the two guys off and it was just me and Turk, I told Turk if this dude jumps on me you better help. He says, "man he ain't going to do nothing to you, it's all jokes." I go home and I know this guy is probably not joking. I have a few choices, go to school and get my ass whipped, not go to school or go to school prepared. I'm a clever guy, so I guess I'll go prepared. A while ago I had picked that lock box that held that 38 snub nose that my mom pulled on that dude. Me and the 38 are going to school tomorrow. I didn't tell anyone at the time I had the gun. I was only going to use the gun in the case of self-defense. I was waiting to go into my class and here comes Hank walking straight towards me. I'm a little scared not of him, but what I might have to do if he attacks me. We had to wear shirt and ties. He comes up to me and grabs me by the front collar and says didn't I tell you guys not to call me that. I look him dead in the eye and tell him I didn't say it and he better get the fuck up off of me right now. I had already had my hand on the gun in my bag pointed at him. I don't know if he saw the devil in my eyes or what, but he let me go and said don't say it again. I told him fuck you and you better not ever put your hands on me. We starred at each other and he walked away. The whole hallway was crowded and looking on. I went in my class thankful that I didn't have to shoot him. Turk comes in the class and I'm like where the fuck was you at? I told him I was about to shoot Hank ass. He said your ass about to do nothing. I opened the bag and showed him the gun and he said what the fuck you think you are Dirty Benny. We both just laughed. Until this day, Hank doesn't even know how close he came to getting shot. That wouldn't be the last time I pulled a gun on a classmate. I don't know what happened but something about the power I felt with my hand on that gun was exhilarating. After that I would sneak the 38 everywhere I went. I didn't want to shoot anyone, but I was never going to allow someone to try to take advantage of me because I was short. I developed a napoleon complex. I was always the smallest and youngest of most my friends growing up. I was an easy target. It was one kid that grew up with me who set his house on fire. I thought he was crazy. One day he hit me, and I was terrified. A guy that grew up like my brother Vince held him and told me to hit him and I wouldn't. I didn't even tell my sister.

I had a German shepherd named king, that was a puppy. One day this kid kicked my dog. I didn't see it, but they told me about it. I told him to get out of my yard. He was taking his time, so I pushed him. He hit and I charged him, took him down and was wailing on him until he rolled me over and bit me on my back. He wouldn't let go until Ann came out and popped him upside his head. After that I wasn't scared to fight anymore, but still something about the power of holding that gun. I would go to the local high schools Crossland and Potomac to meet girls, because Carroll was an all boy school. Being though I was driving it was easy for me to meet girls, plus I was also a good-looking dude. I remember an incident at Crossland. This girl that was interested in me and I was not interested in her. She got mad at me and some name calling pursued. I called her a black ugly bitch. She told me that she was going to get her brother and his crew to jump me in school. Now I didn't even go to Crossland, but one of my lil homies Mack went to Crossland and I didn't want him to get jumped. We went to the basketball game and I told him to point this guy out. I walked over to the guy and asked him into the hallway. I showed him the 38 and told him what the chick had said about him getting us jumped. I also told him if anything happened to my lil homie. I was coming for him. He told me fuck her. He said I ain't got no problems with you or your lil homie. We dapped and went on about our business. I don't want to mislead you to thinking I was a tough guy or even looking for trouble, because I wasn't. With that said I just was not going for any bullshit. At some point in time I wanted to get my own gun and stop sneaking out my mom and pops gun. I had a friend Rico who was 21. He was like a big brother. I remember one time we were out and thought we were about to get into some beef with some dudes. He knew I had the gun. He told me to give him the gun and he would do the shooting, but we didn't get into any beef that night. I asked him to go to the store and buy me a gun. We had a gun shop close to our neighborhood. We went and started looking at guns. I was choosing between a Tech-9 that shot 9 millimeters bullets with a clip that held 36 bullets or a Calico that shot 22 caliber bullets and a clip that held 100 rounds. I chose the Tech-9. We were just waiting on the paperwork to get the gun. One day I was driving to the rec to play basketball and I got pulled over by the police. Remember I don't have a license and I should not be driving alone. I told the cop one of my friend's names with a license, but something must didn't add up. Somehow, they called my mom, and she came to the scene. She played along with the scenario I had created, as if she was my aunt and not my mother. The cop didn't arrest me, but he did give me a $500 ticket and told me if I had a license just show up to court and I wouldn't have to pay the ticket. We know I wasn't showing up to court. After that I was scared to drive. My mom told me the chances of seeing that cop again was one in a million. I saw the cop two days later at the local pizzeria. I walked home and told my sister to go and get my car. I still drove after that, but I was always paranoid.

My first time getting into the dope game was with an associate of my sister's Roger. We were going to do a 60-40 split in favor of him. He gave me $500 worth of cocaine. I owed him $300. One of my sister's girlfriends dated this dude that got high. My sister let them know and they called me. He told me if I bring him a $50 rock. He would pay me $75. By the end of the night he had brought up everything I had. The next day I called Roger to get some more. He was surprised how fast I moved it, and told the numbers where changing to 70-30 split in his favor. I told him no thanks. I had a few dollars saved plus with the money I made. I paid the $500 ticket. I told my mom my sister gave me the money, because my sister would look out for me while my pops was gone. When she went to the mall shopping, she would always buy me something, like shoes, sweat suit, etc. Not sure if my mom and sister ever discussed it, because around this time things had begun to get weird in my household. My mom had gotten a job something she never had. She was always a stay at home mom. Well she did have the jewelry and clothes business but that didn't work out. One day some strange man called our house and asked for my mother. I asked who he was, and he told me to put my mother on the phone. I told him fuck him and don't ever call here again. At this time, me and mom's relationship had become strained and I didn't know why at the time. I was running wild and she was hardly ever home. He called again and I did the same thing. My mom told me if I could not answer the phone correctly and be respectful, she would punish me. I looked at her and told her as long as you tell my pops why you're punishing me, I'm fine with it. I knew that something was going on with this guy and my mom and I was furious. Here my pops was sitting in jail for taking care of us, and this is how you repay him? A couple days later I got the Tech-9. A couple of days after that I was down in the basement and I heard a horn blow. The Mercedes has a very distinctive sound. I knew it was my mom's horn, but I could hear her walking around upstairs. I went outside and saw this guy sitting in the car that my pops had bought. I was furious and started to call the guy names and telling him to get out of the car. He said little boy go in the house. My mom comes out telling me to go inside. I have always been respectful to my moms, but something inside of me snapped and I told her fuck you too. The guy goes to get out of the car, and I kicked the door on his leg. He screams like a bitch. Rico and Fats were sitting in the basement and came running upstairs. I was about to head to the trunk of my car, because I was about to kill this guy. They grabbed and wouldn't let me go. They were telling me to calm down and I couldn't do what I was thinking, not here, not like this. Like I said, Rico was like a big brother always looking out for me. I knew where the guy lived because I was told my mom's car was parked where he lived. I told him tonight was his last night on earth. I went in the house and into the basement. I don't know what my mom said to my sister, but she came downstairs pleading with me not to do anything. She was crying and telling me she didn't want me to end up in Jail like Darrell. She made me promise I wouldn't do anything. I promised and gave him a pass. That Sunday we went to see my pops and I so wanted to tell him what was going on, but also didn't want to be the cause of him and my mom separating. I thought maybe she will leave this guy alone.

On the visit my pops asked my mom where is she in the morning when he calls? She said she'd be sleeping. He told her "Look I know you might have a boyfriend, but you have a decision to make when I come home." I was shocked, upset and so many things at that moment. How could he be so calm and understanding. We went home that day not saying a word to each other.  It was the summer before my 10<sup>th</sup> grade year and I was trying to see if I even wanted to play football anymore. I had fallen in love with this game and now I just didn't know. Football practice started and some sophomores had the opportunity to make varsity. One of the varsity coaches took a liking to me. He asked me did I play last year. I told him I had to quit because of grades. He liked my play, but they picked some sophomores that were standouts from the freshman team the year before. On the junior varsity I was getting frustrated again. They had me in the tackling line on defense. I was a good tackler and the JV coach instantly took a liking to me. I was never scared to tackle anyone no matter how big they were. When I played little league the older, bigger guys would make me tackle them and tackle me to toughen me up and make me better. This came in handy, but I didn't want to play defense. Once I really knew the coach liked me because of my toughness. I asked him could I get in the running back line. He said he wanted me to be his defensive guy, but he let me go in the running back line anyway. I had some really good runs and he was surprised. I would earn a starting position on defense and offense.  I played both ways and after a couple games I asked if I could just play on the offensive side of the ball. He agreed and I began to do my thing. The Varsity coach that took a liking to me would come to me and ask me how many touchdowns I was going to score, and I would call out 2 or 3. That year I received one of MVP awards on my team. I was happy to be back in the spotlight, but something was missing.  I didn't have that love anymore.

I was exploring trying to get back into the dope game. My sister was dating this dude. I'm not going to even give him a name. We will call him BB, which stands for bitch boy. At the time I thought he was cool. He used to run with one of the biggest drug dealers in the city Ray. I'm not giving him too much attention either because he told on some people I love. Anyway, BB was talking about he could get me some work and we could

22

get some money together. He was never able to produce. He told me he had some family in Woodbridge V.A., and we could make some money if we could get some coke. I was baffled as to why he couldn't get any. I went to one of pops old friend's Nicky. Nicky use to work for my pops but was doing quite well for himself since my pops was gone. He told me he didn't want to do it, because if my pops found out he would kill him. I told him he would never hear about it from me. He also explained that he didn't sell coke, he sold heroin, but he could get me some coke. He got me some coke and it turned out to not be good. I told him and he told me to bring it back. He hadn't charged me any money, so it was no big deal. He told me if he ran across some good cocaine he would call me. He warned me to be careful and told me if I had any problems to let him know. Now the search was on to get some coke.

# Chapter 4

# **The Hustle Begins**

My sister Ann use to play middle-man. She never actually sold any coke to my knowledge, but she would get some and give it to an associate to sell and they would divide the profits. I asked if she knew anyone. She reluctantly told me about a dude I knew named Jerry. My sister was a popular girl because she was pretty, dressed fly and had a nice car, but didn't take any bullshit from anyone. She always had a job since she was 15. I always said that was the difference between her and her brothers. She put me in touch with Jerry who knew me from my days of playing little league football. Most of the older kids on the little league teams always liked me because I was never scared to go up against the older or bigger kids. Jerry agreed to meet with me. He told me he could give me an ounce of powder cocaine for $800. I went to BB and told him I could get an ounce for $1,200 and asked him if that would work. He told me yes, he could give me $2,000 back. Jerry told me to meet him at this nursery. At first, I was like wait a minute. He laughed and told me it wasn't that type of nursery. This is a place where young trees and plants are grown. We met and he gave me the cocaine on consignment. Consignment is when you don't' have to pay any money up front. I gave it to BB that Friday and that Sunday he gave me $2,000. I was sixteen years old and I had just made $1,200 by simply picking something up from one dude and giving it to another dude. I called Jerry to pay him and he was shocked how fast I paid him. He said dam Lil B you moved that with the quickness. I really didn't like people calling me lil Benny. I already had my napoleon complex I was dealing with. This went on for a couple weeks until BB asked me if I could get two ounces. I asked Jerry for two ounces and he said yes with no hesitation. I got the two ounces and gave them to BB that Friday. He called me Monday and told me he had $4,000 and for me to come and get it. He was down in Woodbridge V.A. It was about a 40-minute ride without traffic. It was kind of late on a school night when he called, but there was no way I was not about to go and pick up this money. Once again, I'm thinking how I just made $2,400 playing middleman. I was always a flashy kid, I mean our parents always brought us the top name brand clothe, shoes etc; Now I got some thousands and I began to splurge on myself. I would go to the mall and spend thousands of dollars with no hesitation. I remember buying a rhinestone jean Jacket that cost $1,100. Whenever I went to the mall shopping, I would always get Ann something as well. She had always looked out for me when she went shopping, so now little brother had to return the favor.

The year was 1989 I was a junior at Carroll and it was time for football season. I was really torn about football because I really had lost my love for the game and was falling in love with the dope game. My pops came home on a furlough. A furlough is when they let you come home for 5 days, because you're about to be released. My varsity football coach whom had taken a liking to me when I was on JV called my house to find out if I was OK. My pops asked me what was going on with football and I told him I was not going to play anymore. He told me if I did not play football that I couldn't live in his house anymore. I looked at my mom and said "he's crazy." My pops got mad and charged me. We began to wrestle until I got him up off of me and ran out of the house. He jumped in the Mercedes and chased me down the street and ordered me into the car. I told him I would not get into the car, because I feared he would hit me. He screamed again "get your ass in this car." I walked over and got into the car. We drove back to the house. Once inside he said he couldn't believe I hit him, to which my mother said "that boy didn't hit you, but he got you up off of him." My mom told me to go to my room so they could talk. She told him that he shouldn't try to make me play if I no longer wanted to play. He told her if this boy doesn't play football he's going to wind up in these streets. Little did he know it was too late. That night I drove my pops to meet a friend of his Donny. He gave my pops some cocaine. I made a stupid comment and told my pops I knew somebody that could sell it for him. He looked at me and snapped. What the fuck you mean you know somebody. He said, "I better not catch you anywhere near any drugs or its going to be hell to pay." I thought to myself that was really a dumb thing to say to him and I just shut up and kept driving. I was having problems out of my Chevy. Probably because I dogged it out. I never checked oil or anything. Just put gas in it and go.

My pops was released to the halfway house in Washington D.C. A halfway house is the last place you go until you're basically free. They house federal inmates. You get to leave out at a certain time and go look for a job. You also have to be back by a certain time. You are not allowed to drive a car while you're in the halfway house. Those months went by and things started to go from bad to worse. I thought everything was about to be back to normal. My pops got released from the halfway house and my mom decided to move in with her boyfriend. Although me and my mom's relationship had been strained, I felt like she was abandoning me. I knew my pops, but we didn't really have a relationship yet. My mom had been my best friend whom I would tell everything. I remember me telling her when I had sex at thirteen. She told me to make sure I wrap it up because everything that looks good is not. She also said don't bring them little nappy head girls in her house to have sex. So now I'm in the house with my pops. He has rules. I have to be in the house on weeknights by midnight and on the weekends by 2 am. I was cool with the weeknights, because I never stayed out late on school nights, but not the weekend. The GoGo didn't get to jumping until one am. The GoGo was bands that played in various areas of the city. All the hustlers would show up in their fly cars and jewelry. The finest girls would be there in hopes of landing a hustler. I had been going to GoGo's since I was eight years old. My sister would go, and my mom would make her take me with her. She would say "he can't go with me, I'm going to the GoGo." My mom would say "if he can't go then you can't go." I was usually a hit at the GoGo. The girls would all say look at little man, he's so cute. My sister was popular, and a lot of the hustlers would always try to talk to her. Now that my mom was gone. I guess I was not the only one that was hurting, although my pops would never admit it. I think it crushed my pops when my mom chose that guy over him. My sister had moved in with BB, so it was just me and my pops. I grew up in the bedroom upstairs, but now switched to the downstairs bedroom with bathroom in it. My luck just kept getting worse, so I thought.

The Nova engine locked up one day because I had not put any oil in it. I knew that was probably the problem, so I went and brought some oil

26

to put in it. Of course, that didn't help. Now I needed a new car. I told my pops I wanted a used Nissan 300zx. He told me the only used car he would buy me was a Mercedes Benz. In my mind, I'm thinking to myself, that's better than the Nissan. We began to search for someone to put the car in their name since me or pops had no credit. At the time it was tax case against my pops that involved my mom and my aunt Mamie. The government wanted to seize our house, the Mercedes and even my dirt bike. They said all these things had been bought with proceeds from illegal money. We went to my sister Bonnie. She said her boyfriend Mitch would sign for the car. I was so excited that I was about to get a Mercedes. That is until it was time to get the car. Mitch never showed up and I was furious. He called my pops and said he didn't feel comfortable signing for a car that cost that much. I believe the price of the car was somewhere between $26,000 and $28,000. He said he would sign for a less expensive car. I think the dude was jealous that this young high school kid was going to riding a Benz in his name and he didn't have one. My pops said I had to get a new car that did not cost over $20,000 and the Nissan was out of the question. I had a few thousand saved up. I asked my mom to try to get me a car. She told me she couldn't, because she had just bought a new BMW. She said she would ask her boyfriend Bo to do it. I was conflicted. I wanted to kill this dude and now I'm going to have a car in his name. I told her fine. We went to the dealership, and while they were doing the paperwork he made a statement that they were taking too long and he had to be at work. I pulled him to the side and told him he better shut up and if he fucks this up, I'm going to fuck him up. I don't' know what happened but he didn't get approved for the loan. All I know that day no Nissan 300ZX. My pops and Mitch found a car that they agreed on getting me. It was a Chevy Cavalier Z24. It was white with tan interior. It looked like some white boy racing car. Definitely not the car of a hustler. I absolutely hated that car.  Once again, my friends thought I was crazy, because most of them didn't have a car and here I am on my second car. I was just a spoiled brat. I didn't play football that year. I told my pops I really just wanted to concentrate on my grades and maybe I would play next year. In the dope game everything was going smooth and steady, until one day my sister asked me about BB. She said he told her he was going to Woodbridge. I informed he It was no reason for him to go, because I had not given him any coke. I laughed and said oh he must be at his house cheating on you. I was joking of course, but before I knew it me and Ann were outside of his bedroom window. He lived with his mother and sister, who both wanted to fuck me. Yes, his mother and sister, but we will get to that later. We were at his window and could hear him and some chick. My sister knocked on the door and no one answered. Then everything got quiet inside, until my crazy sister jumped up and punched a hole in his window. Glass was everywhere and I was scared she might be cut. She wasn't thankfully. He jumped up and was like oh you want to break windows do you. I had no thoughts of him doing anything to my sister. He knew I was a no-nonsense dude when it came to my sister. I told any dude that ever messed with my sister, I don't care what you do just never put your hands on my sister. We went around front and I guess that's when the girl snuck out of the window. It was later said that she cut her back going out that window.

Although me and BB were in business together my sister always told me to watch him. She said he would get jealous when I would buy her things. At the time I didn't understand it or even care. He never said or did anything disrespectful to me. I guess the first sign that I couldn't trust him came one time we went down to Woodbridge. His uncles told us about these two white girls. They said they like to drink beers and then they would probably like to have some fun. My first thought process was I couldn't stand beer. The girls came over and asked if we could get some beer. I told BB let's get some beers and some 7up soda. If they want to drink beers that's on them. We went into the bathroom and poured out the beers and filled our cans up with 7up. One of the girls took a liking to me. She whispered in my ear she wanted to fuck me. I told BB I was going to leave and go get a hotel room and I would be back. I left him and his uncles with the other chick. After me and the girl went to the hotel for a few hours we went back to the house. Everyone was still there. BB asked what I was going to tell my sister. I told him there was nothing to tell her. Now I love my sister to death, but I understand men are going to be men and besides I have no idea what went on or didn't while I was gone. Do you know this clown ass nigga told my sister we met some girls and hung out with them. My sister came screaming at me asking me why I didn't tell her about these girls. I told her look I'm not your man's babysitter and I don't know what happen when I left. When I came back everyone was still there. A nigga that snitch on himself definitely will snitch on you. I asked why he opened his mouth, he said that he thought I was going to tell. I already had told him I wasn't. I think he did it to try to drive a wedge between me and my sister, but it didn't work. Later that day when I got home my pops laid a bombshell on me. He called me into his room, and he said he had something to tell me. He explained that he believed that my mother was getting high. My mom always smoked weed when I was growing up as a kid. Hell, as kid I remember when I was twelve, taking some of her weed and smoking it with my friends. I even smoked some weed with PCP on it once. PCP is a drug that had mind altering effects. I didn't like it either, so I was one and done. He said he believed she was smoking crack. My father had just given my mom some money to buy a new BMW and I know she had left him for another dude. I'm sitting here not knowing what to think or believe. I definitely did not believe my mom was on crack. I called her and told her I needed to meet with her immediately and talk. We met and I asked her was she using crack. She looked at me and told me "hell no, where did I get that idea." I just told her I heard it. She still denied it. Sometime had went past, and the word got out that Bo, her boyfriend, smoked crack. I could only assume that my pops was correct about my mom. I became enraged feeling like this dude got my mom smoking crack. My friend would tell me how they would always see Bo driving my mom's new BMW. She would let me drive it some weekends and I would go to the GoGo like I was a big hustler.

Then one day the bottom fell out. I was home alone about 4 AM when I heard this banging on the door. I called my pops and told him someone was banging on the door. He told me to go and see who it was. They said DEA open the door. I said hold on. I told my pops it was the DEA. He said open the door before they break it down. I opened the door and they had the house surrounded. They were looking for BB. He had been part of this notorious drug gang headed by Ray. They showed me pictures and asked me did I know him. I told the agents no I didn't know the guy in the picture. BB and Ann were staying over my mother's house.

I called my mom and told her that agents had just come to the house looking for some dude named BB. BB and my sister went to Woodbridge where he would hide out with his uncles. How you expect to hide from the Feds 40 minutes away is beyond me but, business was still moving so, it was none of my concern. The Feds came back to our house and this time they confiscated my sisters brand new Nissan Pathfinder truck. It seems that BB had sold something to an undercover officer one day while driving her truck. He knew the guy was an undercover and sold him some fake stuff. They still confiscated the truck. The fucked up thing about it was that BB didn't give my sister a dime towards her truck. She worked every day to save her own money to buy that truck. That's just how the Feds work though. They want to seize anything of value even when they are in the wrong. As I said business was still going well. The hard part was keeping my pops from knowing I was hustling. I loved to shop and buy jewelry. When he would inquire about where I was getting things. I would say my sister or mother bought it for me. He wasn't really talking to either one of them. One day I was visiting with a female friend when I got a call from Ann. She was crying hysterically screaming come and get me. I knew BB must have done something to my sister and I loaded my pistol and went to get her and him. When I arrived at BB's uncle house, Ann opened the door and when I saw her face I was immediately in pure rage. Her nose was swollen like a balloon. I asked where was BB? She replied he was gone. I told his uncles I was going to kill him and went outside looking for him. My sister pleaded with me to leave. After about an hour of waiting and no sign of him I decided to leave. He called me the next day apologizing and telling me the story of how he was defending himself against Ann's attack. I know Ann and yes, she was a hot head and always ready to fight. My sister had also given me the same story. I told her if she was to go back to dealing with BB and anything else happened; don't call me because I was ready to take his life. Around this time, I started hanging with my cousin Black. He was a year older than me and was not in the game. I had some other friends that I hung out with just about everyday; Fats and Philroy. Fats brother was a big hustler at the time, and he looked out for Fats. Philroy's mom and sister spoiled him like my family had spoiled me. This would be the first time I experienced jealousy among friends. I called Fats and Philroy and asked them to go to

Georgetown with me to go shopping. They both said they didn't want to go because they didn't have any money. I called Black and asked him and he said sure he would go. I went and picked him up. I remember going into a popular store called Up Against the wall. They had just got a shipment of a new clothing line called Used Jeans. I brought several outfits and asked Black if he wanted something. He seemed shocked that I asked, but quickly replied yes. He got a couple outfits and we left to go back around the neighborhood. We wound up running into Fats, Philroy and Harry. Harry was Fats cousin who was also hustling. They asked to see what I had gotten. We popped the trunk. One them asked me why did I buy the same thing twice? I told them that was Black's stuff. Harry pulled me to the side and said I wouldn't buy him anything with my money. I told him he did not need not to concern himself with what or who, I spend my money on. Truth be told if they would have gone with me. I would have bought everyone something. I have never been a selfish person and never had a problem looking out for someone in my circle.

I got a call from my sister telling me that the feds had picked up BB. I was like fuck now my operation might be going down the tubes. I actually knew the guys that were selling the stuff for BB. 2 white guys named Jaybo and Beeks. I went to pay them a visit. I didn't know their arrangement with BB. They told me they would sell everything, and he would only give them a couple hundred. I had made a new deal with Jerry. I was getting an eighth of a key of coke for $3,000, that's 4 1/2 ounces. I was paying about $650 an ounce. They were making about $3,500 off an ounce. I told them to just give me $2,200 and they could keep the rest. They were excited to say the least. Money was still flowing, and I was happy. One day after it had snowed. I had my pops Benz. I didn't feel like driving so I let Fats drive the car. I was in the back and all I heard was him screaming my name. He slammed into the guard rail head on. Of course, I couldn't tell my pops I allowed him to drive the Benz, so I had to take the blame and my pops never let me hear the end of it. I was shocked but he ended up buying a Toyota Camry. I didn't understand why he got that car back then, but he was still in the game and didn't want to have a flashy car. I had gotten rid of my Tech-9 and needed another gun. I wind up getting 9mm Beretta.

One day I was taking this girl shopping at Landover mall and I had Black with me. We went in the mall and there were some dudes in the store throwing punches. Black asked me if I knew who the dudes were. I told him no. He told me who these guys were and I told him fuck those guys I got that 16 shot in the car. As we were leaving out the store one of the guys called out to the girl I was with. I turned to look at him and he said what are you looking at you big head motherfucker. I said to him fuck you, you bitch ass nigga. The girl grabbed me, and we began to walk. She was trying to calm me down. I only thought it was five of them. As we walked down the hall the dude screams out did you say something. I turn around to a mob of about twenty dudes, but it's too late to bitch out now. I told him fuck you and your boys I got something for all you. I tried to make a run for my car. I remember hearing someone say don't let him get to his car. They were trying to hit me, but I was ducking and running like I was on the football field. Some guy pushed me from behind I got up and continued to run until someone grabbed me. I was like get the fuck off me. He was like calm down it's me Black. I don't know what happened in that few minutes, but I was glad it was over. I had scraped my knee from the fall. I didn't know what happened to the girl. Black looked at me and said, "we have to get you to the hospital." I looked at my knee and said I'll be fine. He said your mouth fucked up. I touched my lips, and nothing was wrong. I touched my teeth and yep they were loose, so I thought. I guess when I fell my teeth must have hit the ground and two came out and one was loose. I didn't have a busted lip or anything. I didn't want to go to the hospital alone, so I called Ann. I met her and when she saw me, she began to cry. I told her I was alright. Just pray for the dudes that did this to me. She gave me an evil look and told me let's get my butt to the hospital. At the hospital they had to cut my tooth from the gums. Now I'm missing three front teeth. We went home she cooked, and we laughed and joked about my new smile. Deep down inside I was on fire to my soul. Next would be one of the biggest lessons I would learn about self-ignorance. My mom had a Chinese dentist and pops had a Black dentist. They asked me which dentist I wanted to go to and I chose my mom's dentist thinking he could do a better job. He was going to make me a flipper, which is a temporary piece you can take in and out until my mouth heals and I could get a permanent bridge. I told my parents I didn't want to go to school with no teeth. They said I could stay out until the flipper was complete. After a few days the dentist called and said the flipper was ready. I walked in and he pulled out this hideous looking thing. The teeth were big and yellow. I told him there was no way I was putting that in my mouth. We left and I told my pops I would try his dentist. They told me I had to go back to school without my teeth. I did and I didn't get too much flack or jokes. I remember finding out where the dudes that jumped me lived at. One night we were set to pay them a surprise visit and right before we did the police rolled up on us. We had to scatter and I loss another one of my guns. I wind up buying another 9mm this time a glock 17 and an uzi. It was crazy. I went to Woodbridge to a pawn shop. Beeks and Jaybo got one of the guys they used sell to to go in and purchase it. In less than 30 minutes I had a semiautomatic machine gun. Sometimes I did question if I had a few screws loose.

One day I was taking my sister to work, and we saw Bo driving my mom's BMW. My friends had told me they use to see him drive it all the time and for some reason that infuriated me. I told Bo to pull over because I had left something in the car last time I drove it. I told my sister to drive my car. She asked me what I was about to do. I just told her to drive. I got into the BMW and pulled my gun on Bo. I told him to get out and walk and I better not ever catch him driving this car again. He got out and began walking. I told my sister to take my car and I would see her later. My mom called my pops and told him what I had done. When I got home my pops was upset with me. He told me I didn't have anything to do with who my mother allows to drive her car. He told me to take my mother her car back. I said ok, but it was Friday and I was going to be hanging out for the weekend. I'll take it to her Sunday. That Saturday night I was driving in the city. I was speeding and got pulled over by a DC cop. He asked me to get out of the car. He asked me if I drove that fast in Maryland and I replied, No sir. He punched me in my face and said, "then why the hell are you speeding in my city." I was scared, not because he hit me, I thought he might search the car and find my gun. He gave me a ticket and I called my mom to let her know what had happened. Of course, the officer lied and said he didn't' hit me that he just grabbed me. My mom stated he had no reason to touch me period. She asked me if I was ok. I told her the cop hit like a girl. She laughed and said I was crazy, but still her baby boy. I returned the car and apologized to my mom if I caused her any inconvenience. She hugged me and told me that I needed not be so angry. I think she knew I missed her but was also angry. My mom looked like she had loss a lot of weight even though she was always a petite woman. My mom asked would I sell some drugs to Bo, she told me BB use to sell him drugs. I told her no I didn't have anything. I was finally realizing she was on drugs. That day I went home and cried. See although I sold drugs. I never saw the consequences, because I was usually the middleman. I had confided in BB that I thought my mom was using. When I realized he sold to Bo that it was like selling to my mother. I was pissed at him, but he was in the feds and I couldn't have this conversation over the phone. Time went on and I was hating my car more and more. I decided I was going to get rid of my car.

One day my pops asked to switch cars. While he had my car. I had a friend steal the car and set the car on fire. I thought for sure now I would get that Benz. You know my pops bought me another Chevy white Z24. This one had a sunroof and power windows. My plan backfired and blew up in my face literally. It was my senior year and our school was going coed. I remember walking into school and a news reporter from channel 7 asked how did I feel about girls attending classes with us. I told him it was no big deal. We interact with them on a daily basis anyway, so having them in the same class wouldn't make a difference. Oh boy was I wrong it made a huge difference. All the guys wanted to be super cool, everyone was faking like they were hustlers. I just sat back and laughed. I was not fazed by the new girls at my school because, I was getting all the girls at the local high school of Crossland and Potomac. I mean I looked at myself as the prize. I had money, a car and I looked good. One morning while going into the cafeteria before school. A group of us were walking and talking. A guy on the football team walked up and ask what we were talking about. I told him to mind his business and everyone started to laugh. He said that's why you got jumped and got your teeth knocked out and everyone laughed. I went back to my car and got my Glock. I called him out of the cafeteria into the hall and pulled out the gun and stuck it into his stomach. I told him if he ever made a joke about my mouth, I would shoot his fat ass. He started crying and saying he was sorry, and he knows what it feels like to be jumped. I went and put the gun back up. Tuck came out and told me that he had told people I pulled a gun and I should leave school. I laughed and said he won't tell any teachers. Plus, I had a great hiding space for my gun. That's' the only thing I can say I liked about Z24. It had been searched on 3 different occasions by police and they never found my gun.

I never had a problem with getting girls. Girls thought my parents had money and maybe they could get me to buy them things. I remember watching my sister use and take advantage of dudes that thought she was going to give them some sex only to be played like a sucker. I knew I would never allow a girl to play me like that. I did have a steady girlfriend since the eighth grade. She lived around my older sister's neighborhood. Her name was Danni. She probably was my second love after my mom. We were on and off much throughout high school. I had been with some girls from Potomac High School, mostly cheerleaders and girls from Crossland. Crossland was the high school I would have attended if I had not attended Carroll. It was always funny to me how dudes would act like suckers over girls that they thought liked them but would turn around and fuck another dude. It was a particular crew of girls from Crossland that use to hang together. I knew all of their boyfriends and I still fucked all three. Two of the dudes got mad and stopped speaking to me, but I didn't care. The third would laugh when we saw each other. I mean we were in high school and probably not going to marry these girls.

Me and Danni broke up my junior year again. It was like one minute we were together; the next we were not. I soon grew tired of the back and forth, but still had a special place in my heart for her. I really didn't trust too many girls. I knew my lifestyle and I knew any day could be my last. One day I went to my sister Shelly get some cocaine because I couldn't get any. Not sure what I was thinking because she told my father everything. One day my pops was in my room, and called for me to come upstairs. He threw a paper bag at me that had a box of baking soda in it. He asked me what it was. I replied baking soda. For those of you that don't know baking soda is what was used to turn powder cocaine into crack. He asked me if I was hustling. With my head down I replied yes.

My pops was always offering me money and I felt bad taking it knowing I was making money. He said, "why do you take my money if you are making your own money?" I replied, "whenever you ask me do I need some money and I say no, you start to question me about where I'm getting money from, so I just take the money when you offer it." He asked me the two most important things any hustler should know and have. Do you have money for a lawyer and bond money? I had a little money saved up, but never thought about jail, bond, or a lawyer. He told me once again the reason why he did what he did was so that I could have a better life than he did. He told me he wanted me to stop. Unfortunately, it was too late. I actually wanted him to stop. I went back out for the football team and got injured. I could have pushed through the injury, but this was my way out from having to play. I remember not receiving my twelfth-grade schedule, and I was freaking out. Once school started, I went to the vice principal and asked why I hadn't received a schedule. He told me although I was on the honor roll, I was supposed to go to summer school because I had missed too many days during my junior school year. In order to graduate, I had to make a deal to take eleventh grade and twelfth grade English for the first two semesters and pass them both. He was my eleventh-grade history teacher and took a liking to me. His class was right after lunch and everyday like clockwork, I would fall asleep in his class. I always got A's and B's on his exams. He said to me one day, "I don't know how you do it., there is no way that you could be cheating because you sit in the front of the classroom." I explained that I liked history and would go home and read. After the first quarter was over. I went to him and showed I had an A in eleventh grade English and B in twelfth grade English class. He said "fine just continue with your twelfth grade and you can graduate with your class." I could start with my half of day, because I was working. I had told the school that I would be working at my pops friend liquor store. Which I definitely was not working at. Another coke drought had now taken place and neither my pops nor I knew where to get any. For some reason I went to my sister Shelly again. She told me her boyfriend could get me some. I gave them my last four thousand dollars. The coke they gave me was bad. I told them I wanted my money back and they told me they would sell it and give me money. I never got my money and the dude disappeared. I was furious and my pops told me not to say anything to my sister and I didn't. Time went past and I was just going to school preparing to graduate. My prom was a horrible disaster that I would never forget. I went to a tailor to have my prom suit made. The suit started out at six hundred dollars and soon soared close to a thousand dollars. My pops reminded me that this was only for one night. He paid for the suit and rented me a Mercedes. I took my ex-girlfriend to the prom, who was in college now. I had paid for a suit, shirt, bowtie, and cummerbund. On the day of the prom only the suit was ready. I made the best of it and put somethings together. Next, we were supposed to be meeting up with some other classmates for dinner, but we couldn't find the restaurant. Once again, I had to improvise. I went to the Market Inn seafood restaurant. It was a place where a lot of politicians and middle to upper class people would eat. My mom and pops took us there often and they knew us. The hostess pulled me to the side and asked me what was going on? I explained we were running late for the prom. He said, "your just in time for your reservations" and sat us immediately. My parents where always good tippers and taught me that taking care of people would always help you in the long run. We finally got to the prom and it was an ok night. I dropped my date off and went out to the GoGo.

# Chapter 5

# Full Time Hustler

It was finally time for graduation, and I was excited to be done with school. My excitement was short lived. I was expecting to see my mom at my graduation. Although I was smiling on the outside. I was angry and crushed on the inside. I couldn't believe she wouldn't show up for my special day. School was over and now it was time to really get to hustling. I didn't usually hangout, but with no school I started going out to the clubs. One of our favorite hangouts was Triples. It was a two-level club. On certain nights they had female strippers upstairs and male strippers downstairs. After the stripping was over, they would turn it into one big club. All the dudes that were getting money frequented the club. I met and fucked a lot of the strippers. My boys couldn't understand how I could get the strippers without giving them any money. There was this one white girl that asked me for some powder one day, I told if she fucked Black and I, I would give her some. Black was always a hilarious character. After we fucked her. Black and her were having a deep conversation where she is telling him about herself and some dudes we knew that had paid her to fuck her. She said she had an orgasm in a dudes mouth from him eating her pussy. We both were like what the fuck. You came in his mouth. She replied you guys just came in my mouth. Yes, but that's your mouth we both thought I'm sure. A lot of the stripers wanted to have more than a physical relationship with me that I definitely was not willing to have. I mean they were some sexy women, but I was not ready to be involved with anyone but my money. My pops called an associate of his named Perry. Perry fronted me a half of key of cocaine. I was grateful for the call, but still upset about my four thousand. My cousin Black had graduated the year before me and was working at the Patent and Trademark Department. He was hustling a little bit at the time. I figured I could work and hustle as well. I applied for the job and took the civil service test. I got the job, but after three days I knew this was not the place for me. I told my pops I didn't like the job. He told me if you don't like the job then quit. I quit that day. The next morning, he knocked on my door and asked if I was going to work. I told him that I had quit. He said I thought you were going to at least work 2 weeks and get a paycheck. I thought to myself why would I do that? Life was going pretty well as hustling went. I had a reliable connect with the cocaine. Me and my pops were starting to build a bond. It was difficult, because he wanted to be hands-on with me about everything I did. One minute he would say to me you ain't no grown man and then the next he would say. You're a man playing in a man's game. I just wanted him to let me do me and respect me. I remember he would get upset when I would hang out with my cousin Kenyon. I called him Fats, because he was a huge dude, but was a year younger than me. Fats was an only child and his mom pampered him. We had been close since we were kids. His mom didn't like him hanging out with me, because of my lifestyle. He would have to

38

lie or sneak out to hang out with me. I also had my nephew lil Benny, he was hustling too. My pops told us both never go to Virginia to sell drugs, because they were commonwealth state and their punishments were more severe. Neither one of us listened and Benny was set up and locked up. He had never been in any trouble in his life. The judge even said if it were up to him, he would not have given him the fifteen years. Under the new law, he would be required to do 85 percent of his time. That was my wakeup call and I never took drugs into Virginia again. I still used to go to Virginia to hang out at the football games. One day while I was down there, we were out front throwing the football. I noticed a white guy sitting in the car a few houses down. I asked Jaybo and Beeks who it was, and they said they had no idea. We all went in the house. Jaybo left to get us some chicken. Someone called the house and said the police had Jaybo on the side of the road. His brother wanted to go and see what was going on. I remember when we walked outside, I noticed the car was gone. We all jumped into my car and when I got to the stop sign I looked left and saw the guy in the car. I told them I don't know what's going on, but the police are about to jump out on us. Seconds later they came from everywhere. They took me out the car and handcuffed me. The lady leading the search told me she heard that I was bringing all the guns and drugs into her city. I told her I had no Idea what she was talking, and I was terrified of guns. I told her that if I had a gun, I would probably shoot myself in the foot. I was a little nervous, because I did have a gun in the car. They searched my car and after the third time I felt like they were not going to find the gun. I began to get cocky. I began to tell them my uncle was a lawyer and I needed some names, because someone is going to lose a job. They finally uncuffed me and let me go. I left Virginia and it would be a long time before I returned. It was the weekend and me, Fats and my other cousin Tank were heading out for some fun. Tank was older than me. Tank use to hustle but the Feds came to his house one day looking for another guy who had used his name. After that, Tank got scared and got out of the game. We were not close growing up, but now we were starting to hang out more. One night me, Fats, and Tank were riding through the city. Fats was in the front passenger seat. He looks at me with a stupid look and says the dude in the car next to us called him a fat motherfucker. I started to laugh. Tank asked if I had the gun in the car. At the time I had the Uzi in the car. I told him yes. I thought he was just going to scare the dudes. He started to tie up his hoody. I asked what are you about to do? He replied that he was about to shoot the dudes. I told him to calm down and put the gun away. I said he is a fat motherfucker and began laughing. I loved Fats, but this was not the time or place for this.

The year was 1991 and I was going up and down with the hustling. I had about eighteen thousand dollars. I was really tired of the Z24 and wanted a new car. Nissan had just come out with a white SUV with leather seats called Nissan pathfinder. My sister had a pathfinder. That's the truck BB had got taken from her. Me and Tank saw the truck on the same day. When we talked that day, we both talked about buying the truck. Tank's neighbor Frenchie worked at a Nissan dealer. Tank wound up getting the truck first. I thought to myself I couldn't get the same truck, because the truck only came in one color with the leather seats. I called Mitch and asked would he trade my car in if I gave him some money. He agreed and I told Tank to tell Frenchie I wanted to get a 91 Nissan 300zx. I met with Frenchie and told him I didn't want a car note more than $500. He ordered me a black metallic 2+2. I gave Mitch $2,500 and had put down $9,000 down. I knew nothing about financing, interest rates, or anything when it came to purchasing a car. After they tacked on money for paying off the Z24 and an interest rate of 23.9 percent. My car note would be $749 a month. That was not what I had discussed with Frenchie. I looked at the car and I thought to myself if I couldn't come up with a thousand dollars a month for a car, I wasn't a good hustler. I told Mitch to sign for the car. I had the fly new sports car with the T tops. Of course, my sister Shelly told my pops I had gotten a new car. He told me to bring it pass so he could see it. He asked me what my car note was. I lied and said $500. He screamed five hundred, are you crazy. You're going to have to hustle like hell to keep that up. Imagine if I told him the truth. He also asked me had I paid Perry. I told him no, but I had his money. He told me to make sure you always pay the connect first in case something happened, that way you could always get some more. Plus, you don't want him to think you took his money to buy your car. After I bought the Z, business started to boom. Pops had introduced me to another associate named Whitefolks. I already knew him because he owned the liquor store, I said I worked at in high school. Now he was supplying me coke as well. I remember going from $9,000 to $50,000 dollars in just a couple of months. I had finally convinced my pops to stop and I told him that I would take care of the bills at the house we had in Maryland.

My sister Shelly had suffered a brain aneurysm. They told my pops and her mother that she would not live until the morning. She lived until the next morning and 17 more years after that. I always said doctors are just practicing and they never know for sure. Her, my nephew Eric and my niece Jewel all came to live at the house. Me and my pops were slowly, but surely building a relationship. He didn't like some of my ways and was schooling me to the game of life in the streets. One of his pet peeves was that I always carried a gun with me no matter where I went. My motto was, 'if my gun can't go, then I can't go." One day he asked to use my Z and I threw him the keys. About ten minutes later he came back and asked did I have a gun in the car. I was like, my bad yes, I do. He screamed at me that I didn't need to take that gun everywhere. I took the gun out and gave him the keys and he left. He just didn't understand. Times had changed and there was no honor in the streets. Everyone wanted to do something to you because they were jealous. I was not a guy that went out looking for trouble, but I was not going to run away from it either. He would also get on me constantly about wearing a hat. I was not fond of hats because I always had a fresh haircut. My pops told me I looked too young to be driving that expensive sports car. I always looked young for my age. He thought a hat would make me look older and police would not focus on me as much. I told him I heard wearing hats made you go bald early. He replied, "I wear hats every day." I looked at him laughed and said, "yeah and your ass is going bald." When I got my car back from my pops it was a hat laying in the passenger seat which I never wore.

Atlantic city was a place most of the hustlers went to gamble. My pops had contacted one of his connects from New York and we were going to meet them to discuss some business in Atlantic City. I took ten thousand dollars because I figured we would do some gambling as well. Once we arrived the connect told my pops they would not be able to make it due to some family emergency. We decided to stay a couple days and relax. I remember my pops was an out better on the crap table. He liked to bet the dice don't pass once you caught your point. He would lay odds, and when you would miss your point he would win. After a few days we were broke. I wanted to shoot the dice, but he said that was not a good bet. I got a phone call from one of my customers, Honey. She was actually one of my pops customers that he had given to me when we decided I would take over the family business so he could retire. Honey lived in DC and was visiting Atlantic City. I had told her I was going to be heading up for a few days. She told me to come over to her hotel. I met her at her hotel, and she told me she was going to play roulette. I told her I was broke, and I didn't know how to play anyway. She had owed me some money and gave me $500 and told me to go and play with her. Reluctantly I went with her to the roulette table and started placing bets. I turned the $500 into $2,700. I immediately went and got my pops. I told him I had $2,700 and I wanted to go to the craps table and shoot the dice. I told him he could make the bets, but I was going to shoot the dice. He agreed with a smirk on his face. I shot the dice and we turned that $2,700 into $9,000. We were basically even. At the time we were not getting rated or comped. My pops said he was tired and wanted to head to bed. I told him I was going to a night club. I walked back past the crap table and decided to make some bets. I would lay odds when people caught the point of ten or four. You have to lay two to one odds. I would put up $500 to win $250. In Atlantic City they have a lot of vagrants in the casino begging or trying to give you advice in hopes you win so then they can beg you for money. This guy told me I didn't have to wait until they catch their point to lay odds. I managed to turn that $9,000 into $300 dollars. I was devastated and knew my pops would be pissed. I went to the room and he was sleep. When I came in the room he rolled over and said, "You lost all that money didn't you?" I said "yes," and he rolled over and went back to sleep. I was like how the hell did he know. The next day we were getting ready to leave and I tried to go to the crap table. He screamed at me to bring my ass on. He stated we had the money back and you went and loss it. In my mind I was like it was my money to lose, but I didn't say a word. That was a long drive home of mostly silence. The next day a female friend of mine named Karen asked me to come over her house.

We had become pretty close friends. We used to mess around a bit but were more of friends now. I knew she had a boyfriend, but I didn't care. We were watching tv when someone knocked on her door. She looked at me and asked me to be quiet. I was dying laughing inside, because I knew it must be her boyfriend. She turned off the tv and took me into her bedroom. I asked if she wanted me to leave. She told me no and that he wouldn't do anything to me. I pulled the Uzi out of my pants and told her I know he's not going to do anything to me. She looked at me like I was crazy and smiled. I think she liked this type of drama. Her boyfriend called and left a message on the answering machine. He said I know you got somebody in there and I coming through your bedroom window. She lived on the top floor. I asked who does he think he is Tarzan? She laughed and the next thing I know we were having sex. She told me he said to her that she never answers her door when the Black Z is outside. That was the last time I went over her house. I was not scared of him, but I was scared of what I might do if he did something to my car. We remained good friends, but as I stated I never went back over her house. It was a cool summer night and me and Black were at my house chilling when I got a call. It was dude that owed me a few dollars. I told Black to ride with me. As we were leaving out the room, he asked me was I getting the gun. I told him no. I was only going to meet this dude and come right back. He looked at me and grabbed the gun anyway. At the time the only gun I had was the Uzi. After I picked the money up. I was heading home. I remember passing this old beat up car. The car seemed to start to follow me, so I sped up. It seemed the faster I went the faster it went. Eventually the car started to pull up beside me. I slowed down so I could see what was going on. It was the police and they demanded that I pull over. Once I pulled over, three officers got out of the car with their pistols drawn and ordered me out of the car. Black was still sleep. He said he remember waking up with a pistol in his face, but when he saw it was a white guy he knew it was the police so he was fine. The white officer searched my car and found nothing. Then the Black female officer searched the car and she also found nothing. The Black male cop was like I know they got something, and he searched the car again. He pulled out a black trash bag. I just put my head down because I knew what was in the bag. I looked at Black and told him that I would take the responsibility for the gun. He looked at me and said shut up don't say anything. Now I know a whole lot of dudes who would have just let me take that charge, but not Black. That was the moment we became closer than brothers and there would be nothing I wouldn't do for him after that. They cuffed us and took us down to the station. While we were at the station Black was his normal joking self. I mean were just got caught with an Uzi and he's playing with the police. One cop came to our cell and asked us where we got it. Black replied; give me a hundred dollars and I'll get you one. I didn't think the shit was funny, but him and the cop laughed. Black was even flirting with the lady cop that was processing him. Everything was fine and funny until they told us that one of us had been denied bond. We looked at each other and they said Thornton you're good and Greenfield denied. See we both had used Ann as a contact to verify who we were. She did not answer the phone, but I had my driver's License so they could verify me, and Black didn't. I was laughing with the look on his face. He said call my mother, call my mother. When I got out. I called Ann and she came and picked me up. We waited around for Black, but we couldn't find him. When I got home my pops was waiting for me. He looked at me and shook his head. I told you about them got dam guns. Now your ass going to jail. I just kind of shrugged my shoulders. I was pissed that they had taken my Uzi and impounded my car. I was even more pissed when I got my car out of the impound. They had flattened all my tires, written on the hood of my car with chalk, and stole all of my music tapes.

I was referred to this lawyer whom was not really a defense attorney I believe, but he took the case anyway. I paid for Black's lawyer as well. That was the least I could do. Other than that, everything was going great. Money was flowing, I had the pick of any girl I wanted and just loving life. I also love the fact that I could do things for my family. That's what money has always been about to me; helping others. Black caught another gun case in Maryland and got Bobby Lakes to represent him. Bobby was a funny dude. He thought he was so cool, but his ass was true to what they say about lawyers -- definitely a snake. I had a lot of cousins all over the city and in Maryland. I was always trying to make sure if they wanted to get money I would look out for them. One particular cousin, Pierre was a continuous fuck up. We had hung out as kids and played on the same little league football team. We had strayed apart because he was always in the middle of some bullshit ass drama. He called me up one day and asked me to front him some coke. I went to meet him and told him; look we family but don't fuck up. He said he wouldn't fuck up, so we started to get some money together. We were at the carwash and I told him to get the gun from under the floormat because they pull the floormats up when they vacuum. When we got outside waiting on my car, this dude that was getting his truck washed started to look at us strange. I asked Pierre did he know him, and he said no. The guy pulled off, but he kept riding back pass. I told Pierre to pass me the gun in case this dude was about to try something. My car finally was ready. We got into the car and drove off. It was weird because the guy never said anything. The next day Pierre told me that he knew the dude's name and where he hung out at. I was curious how he knew this, but I didn't even bother asking. That week at a basketball game I saw this same dude with a bunch of dudes. I thought for sure they were going to jump me. He looked at me as if he had never seen me in his life and kept walking. Later Pierre informed me that this dude had bought a black car just like mine. We ran into this guy again and this time he acted like he wanted some problems. He started following me until I pulled into an alley, cut off my lights and jumped out the car. He immediately backed up and went the other way.

It was another drought and Pierre told me he knew a guy named Frank who had some coke. I figured that he wouldn't put me into any bullshit, because if I make money, he makes money. Frank told me he knew some dudes in NYC and he could get us some good coke. He said he would drive the stuff back to Baltimore. I figured if he brought it back to Baltimore I was practically home. Of course, the coke was no good and I wanted to kill Pierre and Frank. Frank was down in North Carolina and I told Pierre I wanted us to go down to North Carolina to confront Frank. He declined and that began to dissolve our relationship in business. He was family so I couldn't do anything to him. My father's friend Whitefolks had finally got some coke and I was back in business. After that he would always alert me of when there was going to be a drought and even if I didn't have all the money, he would give me some coke to hold me over.

Me and my pops where still trying to build a relationship. He just saw me as reckless kid destined for trouble and to be honest, I was. My Napoleon complex caused me to think and act irrational.

There was this guy who lived around Black's neighborhood who owed me some money. One day I go around their neighborhood and they are outside gambling. I tell Black to get in the game so the guy that owed me money would not leave. I go to my car and get my pistol and come back and pistol whip the dude. Black is grabbing me and asking me am I crazy. I mean it was in the middle of the day and everyone was outside. I told him no one is going to owe me money and just gamble in my face without paying me. He asked me how much the guy owed me. I told him $300 dollars. He looks at me and shakes his head and says. They were gambling for a dollar. I told him I don't give a fuck and laughed, we got into the car and left. I don't know if the guys in Blacks neighborhood like me and I didn't care. I was supplying some of them with coke and was not going for any bullshit with my money. One day a couple guys challenged me and my friend Fats to a basketball game, not to get him confused with my cousin Fats. It was a two on two game. I think we played for fifteen hundred. A few guys from Blacks neighborhood put the money up against me. We were down and looked like we were going to lose when I went up for a rebound and I twist my ankle. I told them I couldn't play because of my ankle. One of the guys said if he can't play then he is just going to have to pay. I whispered in Black's ear that I was going to my car to get my 36 shot and if dude had a problem it would be solved. Tank was also with me and ready for whatever, but cooler heads prevailed, and nothing happened. We never finished that game and they never got paid. I probably was wrong, but I didn't give a fuck. My pops was hearing about me doing crazy things. Once he decided to retire and let me take over. He began to funnel me his clients. One particular client of his Jerome owed me $1,000. I put word out I was going to shoot him or his car whichever one I saw first. He immediately went to my pops and told him to talk to me and that he was going to pay me. My pops called me up and said we needed to talk and told me to meet him at the skin house. They had crap houses all over the city, but my pops loved to play a game called Georgia skin. We would rent a house and have skin games there. It was tens of thousands of dollars won and loss in the skin house. Once I arrived, he told me to come upstairs so we could talk in private. He explained to me that the way I was conducting business was wrong and that I would not last long. He stated either I'm going to kill someone and go to jail or someone was going to be scared and going to kill me. He gave me a scenario. He said, "say a guy owes you five thousand dollars and you shoot and kill the guy." Say you only get five years. He said you know how many times you can make five thousand dollars in five years. He stated this is business and no one forces you to give anyone something on consignment. That's a business decision you made and sometimes you will make bad business decisions. He said never consign something you can't afford to give. He said on a different note you never allow anyone to take anything from you. He said if someone takes something from you. You come and get me, and we will go kill them together. This day and those words saved my life, because he was absolutely correct. I was headed for disaster. We never discussed what I was getting or making so he thought I just blew all my money. I remember when I made my first $50,000. I was so proud of myself. I was like shit I'm only 19. I knew other dudes had more, but I never concerned myself with the next man.

Another important thing my pops had taught me. Mind your own business and the business that pays you. He said you can't make all the money. You have to allow the people you deal with to make money too. They will be loyal and faithful as long as you look out for them. I always made sure anyone in my circle made money. One day me and Black came into the house and my pops told Black he wanted to talk to him. He told him to talk to me and tell me to stop blowing all of my money. Black came downstairs laughing. He said you and your pops don't talk about your money, do you? I told him no why? He said he thinks you just blow all your money. When it came to money, we never discussed it, but it has never been an issue between us. Whatever he needed he could always get, and he did.

# Chapter 6

# **The New Hustle**

My pops loved to gamble and pulled me into it. It would be my downfall several times. I had asked him about sports betting. He had told me that I should never do it. Of course, I didn't listen and over the years I lost hundreds of thousands of dollars. I remember one particular incident that I owed the bookie $9,000 and Tank owed the bookie $4,000. Now Tank worked at Saks and didn't hustle, so I really didn't know how he was betting, but he was. On the day we were supposed to pay the bookie he came over my house, but today something seemed wrong. He was pacing back and forth. I asked him was he ok. He replied hell no I ain't ok. I don't have $4,000 to pay the bookie. I just sat there like oh shit. He told me he had an idea. He said we could kill the bookie instead of paying him. I told him no, that would not be cool. He told me he would do it and I didn't have to do anything. I told him no again. I'll pay your money you just can't bet anymore. I wonder does the bookie know how close he came to death because someone owed him money.

Although my pops didn't want me to bet with the bookie. He had no problems with me playing skin. Well as long as he was there to make sure I would not get cheated. He only liked me to gamble under his supervision. I would have to sneak to crap games. I remember one day I was in the crap house and I was winning about ten thousand dollars. He came in looked at me with fire in his eyes. Although I was winning. I knew it was time to leave. He warned me about gambling in the local crap houses. He said if you win a lot of money guys might try to rob you. He said if you are losing a lot, guys will think you have money and still try to rob you. I was not worried about either, but I did take heed to his advice. I was always strapped, and I mean always strapped and was never worried about being robbed. The skin house had some crazy scenarios that took place and was full of characters. Mostly were older gentlemen, but some young guys had also taken a liking to the game. I remember one older guy by the name of dog who use to pee on himself. He could not sit in chairs with cushions. He had to use the metal folding chairs. One particular day I came into our skin house and Dog was sitting in a chair. He asked if I wanted his seat because he was not playing. I said sure until he got up and I saw a puddle in the seat. He said oh shit I pissed in the chair. I told him no worries just take the chair and I'll stand. One day an argument broke out between Dog and another old guy named Bud. Bud was a cool old dude that would lend and borrow money when he got drunk. If Bud borrowed some money from you, he would typically pay you the next day. Dog told Bud he owed him some money, but Bud told him he didn't. It was at the end of the night and we were about to close up for the night. The argument seemed to get heated, but I didn't think too much of these dudes who were seventy plus would come to anything more than words. Bud walked funny because he had his hips replaced. I jokingly told them to quiet down and take the argument outside. When they got outside. Dog hit Bud and Bud fell like a sack of potatoes. It was one of the funniest things I had ever seen in my life. Dog took off running. Bud got up and tried to run after him, but the hips wouldn't let him. The next night Bud came to the skin house he had blood dot in his eye. I teased him all night. I told him my main man Dog told me if he gave me any problems to call him. He would get mad and say fuck you lil Benny. My pops told me to stop teasing him. Only dudes that knew my father called me lil Benny, because in the streets I went by Peanut. My barber had given me that named because he said my head was shaped like a peanut. When I met dudes in the street or females, I would go by Peanut. Some girls I would give my alias of Anthony. One time not knowing I met two sisters. One of the sisters actually got close enough to know my real name. I was out one night talking to her when the other sister walked up and spoke to her and said hey Anthony. She looked at me and said you fucked me and my sister huh. I told her I didn't know you were sisters. She laughed and said well at least I know your real name. DC was a small city and you were always bound to bump into someone's ex girl. If you were getting money females just sough you out. I was always careful not to get too caught up with DC females. Another skin house incident was one I was involved in. It was a guy named Young. I have no idea why they called him that. I remember the first time I met this dude I thought I was going to have to kill him. I walked into our skin house and he was screaming at my pops. I asked my pops who this guy was, and he told me to pay him no attention. He was just a bag of hot air. I learned he owned his own business. One day he called me and asked me to borrow a thousand dollars. I didn't know him but figured he would pay me. Of course, when the day came for him to pay me, he was nowhere to be found. A guy that bought coke from me actually worked for him. I asked him about Young, and he told me he was a tough payer. Meaning he don't pay people. I told him you know what I'll do if he doesn't pay me my money. He said he would talk to him and he paid me a week later. He had an auto mechanic shop and my sister was having problems with her car. I took the car to him, because he patronized our gambling house. I always paid for the repairs, but she got frustrated and took her car to another mechanic. He told her that she needed work that I had already paid for. I went to see Young and told him about the dilemma. I told him I was not accusing him of taking advantage of me and my sister. I told him his mechanics are saying they are doing work that they are not doing. He told me that was bullshit. I told him I wanted my money back. He told me he was not going to give me a dime back. He said go get your gun, I don't care. I told him I would be right back, because that's exactly what I was about to do. Before I could get out the door, he asked me what did he owed me? He paid me and asked me not to come back. I laughed and said cool. It was funny to see a guy act tough and then punk out.

I had been beating him out of three or four thousand dollars every night for a week playing skin. He made a comment he thought the cards were marked and I was cheating. I told him stop crying and go get some more money. The next night he finally beat me, and I borrowed $500 and told him I would bring it back the next day. That night I felt like I was getting sick. The next night I didn't leave the house. My pops called me and asked me was I coming out because Young was at the skin house and he wanted his money. I told him yes and rolled over and went back to sleep. The next night my pops called me again and told me he would pay the guy. I told him no I was on my way. When I walked in the skin house it was only my pops and Bud in there. He told me I shouldn't have told him I was going to pay him the next day if I knew I had no intentions on paying him. I told him he borrowed money from me and took over week after the day he said he was going to pay me. He looked at me with his usual stern look and said what he does has nothing to do with what you do. I raised you to be a man of your word. I said your right my bad pops. Bud looked at me and said Young said he was going to kick me in my ass. My pops yelled at Bud and told him don't say that, you know how that boy is. Bud looked at me when my pops wasn't looking and shook his head to confirm that Young had said it. Young was known for taking advantage of older dudes. I had witnessed him getting rough with some older dudes. I had already established he was a bitch from the car altercation. I called him later that night and to my surprise he was talking rough on the phone. I asked him what was up. He said what's up is my motherfucking money. I told him to calm down because it took him a week to pay me. He said he didn't remember and all he knew was I better take his money to his shop or else. I started laughing, but quickly replied well we are going to find out what else is. I told him he was a bitch and he wasn't going to do shit. I told him to meet me at the skin house. I went back to the skin house to alert my pops that I was about to do something to this dude, because he threatened me. He told me to calm down. A few hours later he called on the house phone and asked one of the old guys could they get the money from me and bring it to him. I was laughing at his scared ass. Too scared to come in and get it.

For the most part the skin house was full of fun nights gambling and listening to stories from my pops and the old dudes about the streets and just growing up in DC. My cousins would come through on occasion and my pops would always get them to play skin. Tank had always talked about being a pimp. I had no idea what a pimp was or what they did. Just they wore crazy looking suits, jerry curls and had nice cars and jewelry. He would say you're going to be a pimp and I would say, shut your ass up. My 300z attracted a lot of attention from everyone, girls, dudes getting money and even the police. I remember one day I was leaving Tanks house and I was driving through the track. The track is where the prostitutes worked. I saw this blonde who looked like a model. She was about six feet tall. She smiled at me, so I pulled over. We began to talk and exchanged numbers. We began to talk and link up for lunch. I knew she was a working girl, but the conversation was cool. One cold night in

November she called me and asked me to meet her. I told her it was too cold outside. She pleaded with me until I met with her. When I met her, she handed me $500 and told me she would call me later. For the next two weeks she would meet me every night and give me no less than five hundred dollars. One day me and Tank where at my house and I told him about her and that she was a working girl. He told me she wanted me to be her pimp. I told him I really had no interest in being her pimp. I was cool with the money I was making and had no problems. I told him she was dealing with a guy from Detroit who was supposed to be a gangster. Although I was not scared of the dude. I just didn't need the trouble. Tank told me that I was going to get her and be her pimp and if the dude had anything to say he would kill him. Tank then told me that I had to serve the pimp. Serving a pimp is when you let him know that his folks, which is the female, no longer wants to be with him and now wants to be with you. He also told me I had to tell her I needed a choosing fee. The money she gave me didn't mean shit. I told her I needed $1,500 by tomorrow to serve him. She was delighted and pleased hearing these words come out my mouth. She told me she already had the money and to meet her to get it. That night we went to serve Detroit J. I had a Glock 9mm and Tank had a 357 Smith & Wesson. Detroit J rolled up in a beautiful, brand new Mercedes Benz. He had two guys with him. I knew it was him because Jenny ran across the street screaming, there he go there he go. I was actually laughing and telling her to calm down and get back to work. They got out of the car and he had a beautiful, long mink coat on, and diamond rings on every finger. I told him my name was Peanut and I was here to serve him. I could tell by the look on his face that he was not pleased. He asked me what was going on and again I reiterated I was here to serve him. He began to talk about she was a dirty bitch and no good and how much money she had made him. He then asked me if she owed me for drugs. I guess he assumed I was a dopeboy. He was not wrong. I actually took offense, because it seemed as if he was not taking me seriously. I asked him if he was accepting the serving or not. He agreed to accept and stated again how she had made him a millions of dollars. I told him cool, now it's her turn to make me a millions of dollars. He then told me she could not work on the track. I laughed and told him he's lucky I let him stay in my city. Me and Tank both had on hoodies and tank lifted his hoodie up to scratch his nose, but I think he wanted to show the 357. They jumped back and I explained that I had come in peace unless you want some problems. We shook hands and went our separate ways. The next night would be the night he felt he was going to test me. He Told Jenny to tell her lil boyfriend he wanted to talk to me. I rolled up on him solo and asked him to pull over so that we could talk. He said I could say what I had to say. I advised him what I had to say he didn't want me to say it in front of his guys in the car with him. He got out and I told him that when I came to him, I came to him with respect. I told him the next time he does or says anything disrespectful pertaining to me I was going to beat his ass. He told me he didn't do anything, and I just said don't let it happen again. I never had any more problems out of Detroit J. Now I was getting Dope money and Hoe money. I know the stereotypical mindset about the world when dealing with working women or escorts. I can and will only speak on my own personal experiences. Now for me this was a business venture and I treated as such. I didn't need to do this, but I chose this business sort of like the guy who runs the brothels in Vegas. Any female I dealt with was of legal age. They were never forced or coerced to do anything they did not want to do. They had freedom and free will to come and go as they saw fit. If they no longer wanted to do business, we always parted amicably. I would even help them in any way I could to facilitate them leaving. We would sit down and discuss their goals and dreams. They had different goals. Some wanted material things such as clothes, jewelry, cars, and apartments. Others were even interested in education to help them in life. Some would want plastic surgery such as breast augmentation etc; We would come up with a business plan and I would help them implement that plan and be successful. I'm not going to say every plan was a success, but I always held my part of the bargain. I got them apartments to work out of and improved their marketing strategies. If they no longer were interested in the business plan we had put together. They were always and I mean always free to go on their way. I just wanted to clarify my role in this business venture.

A week later I was going pass the house we had in Maryland and the police followed me and my pops. I told him they were following him and we both laughed and went into the house. When I left the house, I was surrounded by 5 or 6 cop cars. They told me they wanted me to go down and answer some questions. It was a cop I knew because we went to the same barber. He advised me that I had to go one way or another. I agreed to ride with him. Once in the car I asked him what was going on. He said he did not know. When we got to the precinct, he said they wanted to see me in homicide. Once in homicide a detective came in and started asking me questions. He asked if I knew a guy name Marcellus Smith. I told him no. He asked did I know a guy named Markie and my dumb ass said yes. Markie had just got killed. He asked did I know he had been killed and again I answered yes. He asked how did I know? I said he lived in the area and I just heard it. He asked did someone tell me they had killed him for me. I told him no one has told me or done anything for me. He asked if I had ever been locked up? I asked him what does that have to do with anything? He left and came back and said CPWOL. That stands for carrying a pistol without a license. The current charge that me and Black were facing. I told him look I have no idea what you're talking about or why I'm down here. He asked did I own a black 300zx. I told him My brother in law owned one and let me drive it sometimes. He said that the car was used in the murder. He said Markie owed this guy Craig some money and Craig owed me money. So that's why they believed Markie was killed. I told him that's impossible because the car was impounded when this murder supposedly took place, and nobody owes me any money for anything. He then asked if I knew a guy named Shane. Now I wanted to fuck with his head since he was wasting my time. I said I know several Shane's. Black Shane, White Shane and Fat Shane. He asked me did I know a last name and I said oh no I don't know no last names. He went and checked and saw my story about the impound checked out. I told him I was finished and was ready to leave. I was relieved but also pissed, because someone had tried to implicate me in a murder that I had nothing to do with. I knew it was one of Markie sucker boys in his crew. I told them don't put my name in anything unless they wanted some real problems. They of course denied putting my name in anything.

The next Day I saw my eighth-grade history teacher. She was one of my favorite teachers of all and she liked me because I was a good student.

She told me to follow her to my old junior high. Once there she told me the police had come to school and told them I was involved in a murder and they needed my old address. I told her I had nothing to do with it and that they should have come back to the school to clear my name. She gave me a big hug and told me she cared about me and to be safe. I told her I would, and I left. Weeks were going by and money was coming in from both sides, but Jenny always on some bullshit. I had met another working girl name May. She was Asian with a black girl booty. She said she was not really working much. I told her that the only way we could connect she would have to work fulltime. She was from San Diego and was going home to visit family. She said she would have an answer for me when she got back. I had gotten Jenny an upscale apartment in Virginia and kept her in a fly convertible mustang, but she was starting to play games. She had lied about not making any money, only for me to find out she sent the money to someone. The last straw was when I told her I would not be home that night because I was going to visit my brother Darrell who was locked up. I did not go, and she didn't come home that night. She called and asked what I was doing at the apartment and I asked why wasn't she at the apartment? I told her she must have a bunch of money to be out all night long. She told me she didn't. At this point I decided I no longer wanted to deal with someone I couldn't trust and was over the BS. I called Tank and told him to bring me his truck so I could pack Jenny's things and give them to her. Jenny came to the apartment and caused such a scene, saying she loved me and wanted to be with me and that she was sorry. I told her that I was done. Later on that day when I talked to May, I told her that I was done with Jenny and her bull. May told me she had made a decision and she was ready to be with me and she was going to give me more money than I had ever seen. May was a couple years older than me actually. I mean I was only 19 and she was 21. She definitely knew how to get money though. She was five to six thousand a week. I had a court date coming up for my gun charge. I told her I had never been to Vegas and wanted to go. I got the tickets and we went to Vegas. We stayed at Caesars Palace. The first night I was there a cab driver tried to put me in a scam. May was tired from the flight and wanted to lay down because we got to Vegas at two am their time. I was not going to sleep. I wanted to get out and see the city. I went to one club and couldn't get in because I was not twenty-one. On the way home the cab driver was asking me what I wanted to do. I told him I wanted to go to a club, but not a strip club. He told me he could take me to a club that some celebrities frequent, but it cost fifty bucks to get in. I told him that was not a problem. We pulled up to a club and I paid my money to get in. I walked into this dark room where I was greeted by this hot and sexy blonde. She took me to the bar and asked if I could buy her a drink. I said sure. I didn't drink alcohol at the time, so I got a coke soda. It came up to forty dollars. I was like what the fuck? She asked if I came to party and I said yes not knowing what type of party she was talking about. She told me to talk to the bartender. told me if I wanted to party with one of the girls it would be fifteen hundred. I told him you give me fifteen hundred and I'll go get a girl you can party with. I got up and left out. While I was waiting on a cab. I saw a cab drop some guys off and then get a kickback. I never told May about what had happened.

I wanted to do some shopping, so we went out to the mall. I walked into the Versace store and it seemed liked everyone stopped and looked at me. It was as if I didn't belong in this store. I started to look around. I was looking at this belt and a saleswoman walked up to me and said can I help you. I said yes. I like this belt but it's not my size. She said she would look in the back. I asked her how much the belt was. She said it was a thousand dollars. Now I had bought expensive shoes, suits and just clothes in general. I knew if she came back with that belt in my size, I had to buy it. She came back and said sorry I don't have your size in it, but I do have your size in this one. I told her I didn't like that one. I looked around some more and left out the store. I spent about $2,500 on shopping, but I got much more than just a belt. I never told May about the incident in the club, but when we got home, I was watching 20/20 a news show. They were talking about the place in Vegas. They talked about how men went there and paid thousands of dollars only to be put out of the club after they paid their money. I was laughing on the inside because I knew I would have never paid, but I felt like it was a hustle. That night me and my cousin Fats went out. I told May I would be staying at my place in VA. Later that night she called me to inform me that we had been robbed. I was pissed and told her I was on my way. I had $40,000 at her house and I called her back and asked if they had found my money. She told me no they had just taken my jewelry, clothes and shoes. When I got there, I was even more pissed because she had called the police. They were not going to do anything, and this would have to be something I would handle myself. They asked me the typical questions who and why. I told them I don't know I work at a liquor store. I told them that the jewelry was only worth a couple hundred. My pops had given me the choice on my birthday of two diamond rings he had. The rings were worth $10,000 a piece easily, but it was more sentimental than anything. May didn't feel comfortable there anymore, So I got us a place in Springfield Virginia. It was about thirty minutes from the city. I remember the first time I took Black to see it. He said if someone try to follow you out here, they would think you're heading out of town. It was a nice, quiet and safe place. Right before I started dealing with Jenny, I was dating a young lady by the name of Dana. Our relationship was wild fun and over fast. I saw her with her ex one day and I called it quits. She told me he basically made her take him somewhere when I saw them that day and she was terrified of him. He was about to go to the Feds and do some time.

Everything with me and May was going fine, until I got a call from Dana's cousin, saying she had a baby and the baby was mine. I got in touch with Dana. Me and tank went to see the baby and the baby looked nothing like me. I told her to arrange a blood test and if the test came out that the baby was mine, I would reimburse her and of course start taking care of the child. My sister warned me against it and told me to make all the arrangements. Dana told me the time and the place. I showed up and had my blood drawn with her and the baby as well. A couple weeks later I received a letter stating that the little girl was in fact my baby. I had so many mixed feelings, but knew I had to step up to my responsibility. I told May and I thought she would be upset although all this was before her. She said she would always stand by me no matter what. I started to take of my daughter, and she began to change my life. See my life was always about me, but now I had someone who depended on me and I had to do my best. Me and Dana would argue because she wanted us to get back together and I told her that would never happen. As far as money I told her whatever Brianna needed, I would take care of and I did. Her and May were always at odds and I was always putting out feuds. I went out and got Brianna's named tattooed on my chest. I loved that little girl with all my heart. I would have her with me all the time, but just couldn't shake this strange feeling.  A little while after we had her  one-year old birthday party, I called the place who had done the DNA test. I told them I wanted to do another test but couldn't find her mother. They told me I would need someone from the mother's side of the family to do the test. I told the lady I was just unsure of the first test. She asked me my name and said that's funny my name was not in the computer. She asked for the mother and the child's name and again nothing in the computer. She asked me to fax a copy of the documents I had received. She told me that the documents had come from their office, but her boss's signature had been falsified. I immediately became irate and called my mom whom happen to be babysitting Brianna. I explained what happened she told me to calm down, because she knows my temper. I called Dana and asked if she could leave work. She had been hounding me to buy her a car since I had brought May a car. She tried to guilt trip me talking about my daughter didn't have a car to ride in. I told her I was leaving May and we were going to be a family and I was going to buy her a car. I went and picked up Brianna and then Dana. When we got to her house, I confronted her about the paperwork. She denied any knowledge of doing anything wrong.  I told her that was not my baby and she was a horrible person. I slapped her and I walked out. I went to talk to a lawyer because the only way to get your name removed from a birth certificate is by court order. The first lawyer wanted to throw her in jail, the second wanted to sue her. I just wanted my name off the birth certificate if Brianna was not my daughter. I used a lawyer from one of my gun cases and they did another test and found out Brianna was not my child. I was crushed and once again back in my mind frame where it's only me. Don't get me wrong, I always help and do whatever I can for friends and family, but they are all grown and not my responsibility.

My court date had finally come up. The cops original reason for pulling me over is because they say I was speeding although they had no radar detector. I went to court on the speeding ticket and it got thrown out because no cops showed up. This case had been postponed by the

58

government so many times for about 2 years. They do ⎿
catch another case and they can get you to plead guilty to ⎿
day of court, the government was still not ready. They said on⎿
arresting officers was not there. The judge stated this case has gone
far too long. He asked which officer was not there. The prosecutor
couldn't tell him. The judge said you have thirty minutes to get all three
officers in here or I'm dismissing all the charges. Me and Black both
probably counted every minute.  No officers showed and the case was
dismissed. I was informed during the trial it was a misdemeanor and I
could only get six months if found guilty.  Now I just started carrying my
pistol on my waist. This was the good and bad about this case. After that
case was over, I was relieved that I could go back to being strapped
although it saved me a few times. One day me and Tank were around
Northeast where I had my two apartments. My pops always would put
me up on game. Rule number one never keep any drugs where you live
at.  So, I had rented two apartments. One to keep my coke in and the
other to meet my clients. I would always arrive before anyone I was
meeting so that they never knew about the other apartment. That way if
they ever tried to set me up with the police and they raided the
apartment, there would be no coke. Me and Tank were headed to meet
someone at my apartment. I saw about five cop cars behind us. I told him
I didn't know what was going on, but we were about to be pulled over.
One of the cop cars sped around me and cut me off. They all got out with
their guns drawn and ordered us out of the car. We got out and they
ordered us on the ground. I had a white, brand new Versace outfit and
told them I'm not getting down on that dirty ass ground. They slammed
me up against the car and searched me. They searched my car, but
nothing was in it. I was pissed and was demanding some answers. They
told me someone had just been killed and the person who did it was in a
black car. They were stopping every black car in a five-mile radius. One
cop said they had a witness and we had to wait. The car pulled up and
this old drunk guy got out of the car. He could barely walk he was so
drunk. I said to the officer you have got to be kidding me. He replied yeah,
he is fucked up. He looked at me and immediately said no. He was looking
at Tank for a few minutes. I thought he was about to say some crazy shit,
but he finally said he was not the person either.  After that day we use to

see that guy sitting on his front step a lot. It's funny how you never realize someone until they damn near hold your fate in their hands. Thankfully for both of us we had nothing to do with that murder. The summer was almost over and Me, Tank and Black were enjoying it to the fullest. Black had been talking about getting a new car as well. He asked my opinion on two cars a Honda Accord or Nissan 240. I told him to get the Honda, because the 240 looked like a female's car. He got the 240 and would get pissed when he would try to talk to a girl, and they would ask him if he was driving his girlfriend's car. I just laughed and said, I told you so. We all would be together every day. At night we would ride past the clubs and hang out. Tank would usually drive my car and Black would drive his truck. One night while we were at the club this old dude about sixty hit my car with his van. He was obviously drunk. I immediately took the guns out of my car and put in the truck with Black, so we could call the police. Once the police got there, Tank and the old dude started arguing. I thought Tank was going to hit him and I had to calm him down. I told him I just wanted to get my car fixed. I got the old dude's info and gave him mine. He called me the next day sober and apologetic. He stated, he would like to pay for my car out of his pocket if possible. I told him I would get two estimates and bring them to him. I did and he paid me in cash, and I got my car fixed.

When I was growing up Tone and Vincent were like my big brothers. I was fronting Tone coke at the time. One day when I went to take him some coke. He told me he overheard some dudes talking about some dudes with a black 300zx and another dude with a white Nissan Pathfinder. That happen to be me and Tank. He said the dudes were talking about robbing them. I asked him who the dudes were or where they hang out. He told me he didn't know he just overheard them talking. I was pissed with Tone and told him that when you motherfuckers come. I'm going to kill you all. He looked at me and said what am I talking about. I told him that we grew up like brothers and it's no way I could sit around and hear people talking about doing some harm to you and not find out who and where the dudes hang out. That was the last time I fronted Tone some coke. I told Tank that someone wanted to kidnap and rob us. He laughed and said they would only get pay stubs from him. I laughed, but we knew we just had to stay on point, because this town was always full of jealousy and people wanting to take what you got instead of getting it on their own. My pops had told me he would always support me in anything I did except if he heard I was robbing people. He never had to worry about that because I believed in getting my own money.

I was getting a lot of attention from females just as I wanted by getting the 300zx. Now it was starting to get old and I felt like I couldn't trust most females, plus I had May now who was making good money for us. Everything was going good until she got pregnant. I told her I wasn't ready to have a baby. She was pissed because I was taking care of Brianna when I thought she was mine. I told her I never planned on having a baby with Dana. She got an abortion and I don't think she ever forgave me. It seemed like we were just starting to go through the motions. Communication got bad, to the point where we were barely speaking at all. I was just running the streets more and barely coming home. She really didn't have any problems on the track, because dudes knew I was crazy. Black called me one day and told me he was thinking about buying an Infinity Q45. It was a sweet car. He had actually tried to get me to get the car. At the time I had already had two cars the 300zx and a Nissan Maxima that May primarily drove. I told him that I had some new business deals coming up and I wanted him to become my partner. I needed him to put up some money so we could get some better deals on the coke. The next thing I knew he pulls up in this beautiful Q45. I guess he wasn't interested in the partnership. Our business relationship remained the same, but we became closer than ever. I looked at him like the brother I never had, him and Tank, because me and Darrell really never had a relationship outside of me going to visit him and send him money in Jail. I don't know what it was but after Black got the Q45. It gave me an itch to get a new car as well. May had been trying to get me to get rid of the Z. She said I needed something more luxurious. I looked at a Mercedes coupe and a Lexus coupe. They were similar in price, but the Lexus came with all the bells and whistles. One day me and May where out and I saw this local comedian who was on the rise. He had a white Lexus SC 400 the same one I was interested in getting. I spoke to him and told him he had a nice car. He said thank you. I told him I would be getting one soon. He looked at me with this face of disbelief like yeah whatever dude. I went from fan to thinking he was a fucking clown. Me and Black went to the Lexus dealer so I could see the car. A young white sales lady was helping me. She asked if I wanted to test drive the car. I told her sure and she told me she would be right back. A few minutes later her sales manager came over and told me he could not let me test drive the car. He said because I put on my application that I was in school. I told him that I did not ask to test drive the car she asked me to test drive the car. I told him I just wanted to see the car. He pointed to one on the showroom floor. I asked him was it fully equipped with all the bells and whistles. He told me no. I said the one I wanted to see was fully equipped. I knew what was going on here. He felt I couldn't afford the car. I laughed and I just walked out of the dealership. I brought the Lexus about a week later. I actually paid cash for and put it in Anne's name.

The Lexus didn't look like a dope boy car. Regular chicks were giving me way more attention. I remember this chick flagged me down on the highway. We both pulled over on the side of the road and she offered to take me home and rub me down in a hot bubble bath. I declined, because I didn't trust females. I know dudes who got caught slipping and robbed and killed because a female had set them up. Black and Tank would get upset with me because I would never talk to females when they gave me attention. I told them I'm in a different place and I don't trust most of these bitches. I definitely made it my business to go back to that Lexus dealership. As I pulled up to my delight, I saw the sales manager who refused to show me the car I wanted to buy. He looked at me and said I see you got your Lexus. I said yes and I paid for it in cash. He asked could he help me with something, and I told him no thank you. I was going to the parts department. Of course, I just wanted him to see that I had gotten the car. It was Saturday night, so I was driving past the club. I saw that comedian and he screamed what's up player. I see you got your car. I gave him the same look he gave me when I told him I was getting the car and drove off.

Females in DC were crazy over hustlers, especially if you were moving weight. Dudes were known for buying females expensive gifts, shopping sprees, etc; Not me though, you might get a meal, but no gifts.

I thought everything was going smooth until one day I came home, and something seemed odd when I walked in the door. As I walked into our bedroom, I notice all of May's clothes were gone. I immediately ran to my stash spot in the house where I had $100,000. Not one dime was missing. I called May and asked her what was going on. She told me she was tired of me never being around, and always being gone. I asked her why she didn't have a conversation with me about it. She said I should have known. I told her I was not a mind reader and asked her to come back home. She told me she was ready to move on. I hung up and called Black. I have to admit I was hurt and pissed. I told him May had left and asked if he wanted to move in because I had a two-bedroom, and two bath apartment. He said she would come to her senses and be back in a few days. I told him she was no longer welcome to come back. I couldn't trust her to just leave like this without us having a conversation about her issues before she left. He moved in the next day. He was right she called me a few days later and said she wanted to come back home. I told her that was impossible, because my cousin was now living with me. In the beginning living with Black, was anything but smooth. He still had a room in his mom's house and was treating our apartment like a hotel. Bringing a different girl home every night. I told him that this is where I laid my head and kept a lot of money so he had to keep it down to a couple girls that he could somewhat trust. Things were a little rocky with me and May. One night, Black brought a chick over to the house he had meet while we were out together. He told me I would like her because me she was nasty freak and all the things she had did to him. I laughed at him because I did enjoy a freaky woman. The very next day I saw the girl and her friend. She told me her friend wanted my number so we could hang out. I reluctantly gave her my number. Later that day the girl Black had hooked up with paged me and asked me what I was doing. I told her I was going to get something to eat and she asked if she could come. I told her I would call her back and let her know. I called Black and told him what happened and asked if he liked her. He told me no and to have fun. I laughed and hung the phone up. I called and picked her up and took her out to dinner. We ended up back at me and Black's apartment. She told me she had spent the night last night with Black, but they didn't do anything. She asked me did I know she spent the night. I told her no. I told her me and Black live together, but we are not that close. It's arrangement of convenience. She told me how she liked me much more than Black. I told her cool. She then proceeded to do everything Black told me she did the night before. I was laughing so hard on the inside. The next day I dropped her off and never talked to her again. I met up with Tank and Black for dinner and we all laughed so hard. Tank said when was his turn. About a month went by and I was riding with Black in his van with tinted windows. The girl from that story pulled up on his side and told him to pull over. She's walking up to the passenger side of the van and has no idea that I'm inside the van. When I rolled down the window, she saw me and her smile went dead instantly. She looked at me and said hi. I said to her I have a question to ask you. I said we are like brothers and we won't get mad I promise you. I said we want to know one thing. Who was the best in bed him or me? She was pissed and said fuck you and walked away. I said it's ok I know I was better. Black was laughing so hard and then we pulled off.

I got May another apartment which actually just added to unnecessary expenses, but it was what it was. A client of May's bought her a car. I was pissed because I felt he should have just given her the money, but now she had her own car although she had access to both of my cars at any given time. My gambling was starting to get the best of me. I had met a new bookie name Jim through my old connect Perry. I had stopped betting with my old bookie because my friend Fats ran up a tab and the bookie wanted me to pay for it. I had paid Fats tab of ten thousand because I thought he had the money only to find out he was broke. I told the bookie I would not be covering anymore of his tabs. The first time I bet with Jim should have been my last time. It was basketball season. I met him in the barbershop he worked out of. I told him I wanted to bet two games. I counted out $3,300 twice, a total $6,600. He looked at me strange and then told me he doesn't take that type of action on basketball. He only takes big action on football. He told me I could bet $300 on one game. I gave him $660 and left. I won both games and was pissed. Instead of winning $6,000 I had only won $600. I went to the barbershop to get my money and one of the barbers informed me that he had a heart attack. He told me Jim told him to tell me to come up to the hospital. I went to the hospital and he was in the room with his daughter. She said dad I'm sure he knows you are going to pay him. He told her it was my first-time betting, and he would have my money in the morning when he could get to his property. He paid me the next day. Later that day I got a call from BB saying he was about to be released. Me and Black rented a limo and Ann rode with us to pick him up. While we were driving back, he got sick and threw up in the back of the limo. Once we got back to the city, I gave him some money and told him that he could be my partner. I would get the coke we would sell it and split the profit. I felt I owed him for helping get me started. After a few weeks he told me that he wanted to go and do his own thing. I told him I understood and wished him luck. Football season came around and I was ready to win big. The first week I bet $9,000 on one game and won. I felt like a genius. The next week Jim informed he couldn't take such large bets unless he had the same action on the other side. Once again, I should have quit betting with him.

# Chapter 7

# 7 Hustlers Ups & Downs

The next week I bet three games for $3,000 a piece and loss all three. After that my season was up and down, but mostly down. Between my sports betting and card gambling I was losing tens of thousands on a weekly basis. I was not bringing in enough to sustain the losses. Me and May's relationship was getting worse and worse until we finally went our separate ways. The next thing I knew I was broke, with no money.

I moved back to the house we had in Maryland. None of my connects had any coke. Black had started to deal with this dude named Harry. Harry was the one who said I was stupid for buying Black something back in the day. Harry for some reason was always in competition with me and I believe he was happy to see me down. He told Black to tell me to call him. I told Black fuck him. Black convinced me to swallow my pride and call Harry. I called him and he fronted me some coke. He was talking bad about me to another associate of ours and the guy came and told me. I was pissed and said I was not going to pay Harry because I knew he was a bitch and he wouldn't do anything. Black came to me and told me he vouched that I would pay him, or he would have to. I told him don't ever do that. I paid the dude and moved on. A girl named Terry that I had messed around with when I was younger was back in my life. She was a cool blonde chick who really loved me. I liked her a lot, but I was incapable of loving any woman at the time. I still had the scars of my mother leaving me when I was 15. I always knew I could go to jail and if my mom left my pops and they were married. I just knew a girlfriend would definitely leave me. My brother Darrell had also just been paroled from jail. He came to live with me at the house. Terry was in a car accident and got some money. She gave me the money and along with the money I made off of the stuff with Harry I was able to get some coke. My pops introduced me to this dude named Russ. He was an older cool dude. Things quickly began to turn around for me. I called Russ and told him I wanted a kilo of coke, but I was a couple thousand short. He told me don't worry about it. He trusted me and knew I was good for the money. One day Russ asked me to break down a kilo for him into eighth of kilos, because he couldn't touch it because he was on parole and had to take urines. I told him fine. When I got to my spot and opened up the coke. I noticed it looked like baby powder. I had never seen any good coke look like this before. I bagged up his and took it to him. He called me and told me I had taken too long to bag up the coke and he believed that I had tampered with it because it didn't look right. I told him I just opened and bagged it up. We got into a heated argument. As I was rushing home to check my coke. I called my pops and explained what was going on. I told him the dude had threatened me and that I was not going to allow anyone to threaten me without doing something. My pops told me to calm down and call him after I check my coke. I'm not sure why but that was some really good coke. Russ called me to apologize. I told him I accept his apology, but we could no longer do business. I told him I would never fuck him over, because he always looked out for me. I told him what if someone had actually tampered with coke. You wouldn't have believed that I didn't do it. He told me that he understood where I was coming from, but if I wanted to do business in the future there would be no hard feelings. I told him I wish him the best, but at this time I prefer not to do business. My brother Darrell had made parole. I told him I would pick him up. I rented a limo and got one of the strippers that I knew from back in the days to go with me and surprise him. When I walked into the jail, he said someone said it was a limo outside. I laughed and told him that no limo was outside waiting for him. When we walked outside, she opened the door with a sexy out fit on and said welcome home. He looked at me and smiled. I told him to enjoy himself and I got in the front with the driver to give them some privacy. Darrell had been locked up for eight and half years and I told him it would be some adjustments he would have to make. Darrell was only interested in playing craps in the local gambling houses. We would go in and win thousands in the beginning, but it also comes with some losses. I told Darrell this was cool, but not a way to make a real living. As usual he thought he was smarter than everyone else and would just out gamble them. Things were going ok, but I needed to get away and clear my head. I told Terry that I wanted to take her to Atlantic City for the weekend. They would give me jacuzzi suites with big screen tv's. We had a good time. I didn't win or lose any money. I remember before I left Ann told me not to leave any money around Darrell. I told her my brother wouldn't steal from me. Before I left. I had given him $500 and told him not to go to the gambling house. Just get a girl and chill for the weekend. When I returned, I noticed I was missing $7,000. Before I went crazy, I wanted to look everywhere. The week before I couldn't find my Rolex watch and went crazy only to find it later. I asked Darrell had he seen the money, or did he remember me putting it somewhere else. He told me no and that he had no idea where the money was. I called over the gambling house and asked if they gambled this week. They told me they did, and my brother was losing thousands of dollars. I told Terry to go home. I took the clip out of my pistol and began to pistol whip Darrell. My mom was there and screamed please don't kill him. I told her I was not going to kill him, just teach him a lesson. It was blood everywhere. He ran out of the house. I was so hurt and angry. It was not about the money. If he would have been honest with me and told me he fucked the money up, I could have accepted that. It was him standing in my face and lying. He moved to North Carolina robbed some banks and went back to jail. I felt bad like it was almost my fault, but he is grown and made his own decisions. My pops got me another connect and before I knew it, I had another $60,000. I got me a place back out in VA and brought a 4 door Cadillac Seville. My pops had a two-door green one with a tan rag top. He told me I should have gotten a two door like his.

Me and Terry went our separate ways and I felt like I wanted another working girl. One night me and my cousin Fats went to the Zulu cave. This was a warehouse that they had strippers and anything goes type of place. I remember when I saw her I was like dam she is bad. Her name was Sunny. She was tall light skinned with hazel eyes. She actually reminded me of the former Miss USA Vanessa Williams. I told Fats to go tell her someone important wanted to talk to her. She came over and I was talking to her about who I was and what I wanted with her. She smiled and laughed. The club was over, so I pulled my car up front where all the dancers were leaving out. I called Sunny over to the car. She said nice car. I told her I like nice things and for those around me to have nice things as well. She told me she had some business to handle and I could follow her. I told her after she finished her business to give me a call. She called me and I went and picked her up. I took her to breakfast, and we talked. She didn't really seem interested. I remember taking her back to her hotel and she was snoring in my passenger seat. I thought she must be really tired or trust me. I dropped her off at her room and told her to call me so we could do dinner and get to know each other. A few days later she called me. Me and Fats picked her and one of her girlfriends up. They were both from Wisconsin. We went to dinner and a movie. After that I took them to my place, and we hung out talking. They both seemed to decline my business proposal. Sunny went to sleep on my bed and her girl tried to fuck me. I told her that I was not interested in her sex. I wanted it all or nothing. I dropped them off the next day. About a month went past and I was hustling and still trying to come up with a girl. Sunny called me out of the blue. She told me she was working at club called Macombos in this rough part of DC. She said she wanted to talk to me. Black happened to be with me and was apprehensive about me going to meet her. I told him we were strapped and she's not from here. I called Sunny when I got outside of the club. She came outside handed me some money and put some strange girl in my car. She said she had some more business to take care of and would call me later. As I started driving downtown to drop the other girl off for work, she called out my real name. I turned around and asked how she knew my real name. She said she knew my pops. Her aunt was friends with my pops. I told her this probably would not work. I asked where she wanted to go, and she said to work. I took her down to the track. She didn't get any money and I was actually happy. For some reason that seemed too strange. Sunny called me later and I picked her up. She told me that we needed to talk in depth so she could tell me what was going on with her. She told me she had a son that was about to be two and it was a package deal. He lived with her mom, but she wanted him to be with her once she got established. I told her I agree one hundred percent and asked when could I meet little man? I told her I didn't have any kids and would treat him like he was my own. She smiled and said he was the most important thing in the world to her. I told her then he would also be the most important thing to me. We immediately clicked. She wanted me to meet her family, but she was afraid to fly. She had driven an old beat-up car she had bought from her mom. We drove to Wisconsin in my truck of course, so I could meet her son and her family. She was raised by her step-father and her mom. She had two sisters, one older and one younger and an older brother. Me and her family hit it off immediately. Me and her mom became very close throughout the years. I would often have to call on her when her daughter began doing crazy things. My pops was always down for whatever I was doing, but Ann not so much. Ann always wanted to see me go to college and have a different life. She always said I was the smartest among the three of us and I was wasting my talents. I would just laugh at her and say yeah, I love you too. Things moved fast with me and Sunny. I let her move into my place in VA. I told her that if she wanted a car, she had to get it up. Get it up means you have to make more money than you are currently making. A few months in and everything was going great. One day I wanted to take my pops to Atlantic City so we could relax and do some gambling. I had a great hiding place where I use to keep my money, so I thought. When I returned from Atlantic City. Sunny asked me was I testing her. I asked her what did she mean? She said I had left her in the house with $50,000. I told her no it was not a test, and I did not expect her nosy ass to snooping through my shit. I was pleased that she didn't take the money though. She said she told her friend and she told her take the money and go back to Milwaukee. I asked her why she didn't take the money. She told me she thought that I would be a good influence on her and her son's life. I have to say I was touched, but I did move the money.

I got some bad news. One day my sister informed me that my Cadillac had been stolen. She was using my car and somehow dropped the keys. The insurance company was giving me issues, so I had to hire a lawyer. They tried to say we had something to do with the theft of the car. I told the lawyer that was crazy. The car was paid for, so why would we have the car stolen. Yes, I know what you're thinking, but I liked this car. Sunny had been getting it up and had help me with some other girls. She was really handling her business. I went to this car dealer and brought her a white Mitsubishi 3000GT sports car. I paid $25,000 straight cash for the car. I surprised her with it and she was ecstatic when she saw it. Not bad for her eight months of hard work and dedication. The problem now was that I didn't have a car. I went out and brought me a Jeep Cherokee which I paid $30,000 for. I wanted a Mercedes Benz, but I figured I would wait until I got my settlement from my Cadillac. I had bought both vehicles from the same dealer in VA. I had only given the dealer $25,000 for my truck and still owed him another five. I got a call from BB stating they are raiding our place. I was half asleep and woke up like what the hell. I turned on the news to see that the feds were taking all the cars from the dealership. They said the dealership was supplying drug dealers with cars and not reporting them when they paid large sums of money in cash. I was supposed to go to the dealership that day to give the guy the last five I owed him and pick up my tags and title. That would have been a horrible scene to walk into. I called my lawyer and he told me to come and see him. He told me that he had checked into it and that my truck was on the wanted list. He told me he could take the case for $25,000. I told him I would get back to him. I called Black and gave him my truck to hide around him moms house. Then I went to talk to my pops. I told him what had happened and that the lawyer said he could take the case for $25,000. My pops looked at me a shook his head. He asked me had the feds contacted me or Ann, because my truck was in my sister's name. I told him no. He then said don't go getting a lawyer and start something if they have not even contacted you. He then asked how much I had given the guy for the truck and I told him $25,000 and owed him $5,000. He said there is no way you can know for sure that the lawyer can save your truck. If they take it, you can take the $25,000 you were going to pay the lawyer and buy something else. As usual my pops was right and I was glad I had him to go to. I called the owner of the dealership who I had been dealing with. He told me that my tags and title came in the day after the raid and that if I bring him the $5,000, I could get them. I did and never heard anything from the feds.

I had started to deal with a new connect named Jimmy. Jimmy was about a year older than me and at a different time we dated the same girl. His dad and my pops were associates. I had actually done business with his dad before he passed away. At first, I wouldn't do business with Jimmy, because his prices were always too high. He told me one day he would show me the whip game. The whip game is when you stretch the coke. You may cook up a half a key of coke but get back a half and a quarter which would increase your profits. I told him cool and we started doing business. With the whip game I started to make much more than I use to and was thankful to Jimmy. My pops knew Jimmy's connect and asked if I wanted him to introduce me to him. My loyalty to Jimmy made me say no even though I know that there are times business comes first. I'm not sure what happened, but I remember Jimmy making a comment about how much I was selling and how fast I was selling it and how I was making more money than him. He laughed so I took it as a joke. Later that week I told him I needed to get some coke from him. He told me he would have it and to meet him later that day with the money. For two days he kept putting me on hold. I told my pops and he said he would talk to Jimmy's connect and see if he had some coke. I thought to myself that no way Jimmy's connect has coke and he won't sell me any. My pops came back and told me the connect had coke and would sell it to me. I was torn on dealing with Jimmy's connect, but more torn on not making money. I decided to deal with the connect. Jimmy called me a few days later and we met up. Once again, he made a comment stating I had gone behind his back to his connect and then he laughed and said it's all good we all family. I knew it wasn't good, but now I was like fuck you dude your trying to hold me back for some reason. We talked about meeting for dinner later. We never did meet. DC is a small place and when you are getting money everyone knows it even if your trying to be low key. People know you that you don't know. A lot of people knew me because of my pops. I would go places and people would say that's Benny Thornton's son. Then they would ask is Benny Thornton your father. I would say yes and they all would say, your father is a good man. In the beginning I didn't like it, but as I got older I was proud that my pops was highly respected in the streets.

I knew a lot of the older hustlers because of my pops. They would all gamble together. Some were still in the game and some were out of the game. Just like me some of them had sons who were in the game. One day I was going to get something to eat and I saw this guy named Blow. I didn't really know Blow, but I knew his father. He spoke to me and asked me how I was doing and even asked about my pops. I told him all was good and we shook hands and we went on out our business. I asked my pops if he knew Blow. He told me yes, he knew him, and he thought I knew him as well. He said whenever he would see Blow, he would always ask about me. He also told me Blow was moving major keys of coke. Once again, a drought hit and none of my connects had any coke. The prices were insane, and I refused to pay for anything especially if it was not from one of my reliable sources. I had been burned in the past. I was out one late night and I ran into Blow. I'm usually not the type of guy to just initiate business with someone I don't know. We spoke and I was about to leave out when I said fuck it. I asked Blow if I could speak to him for a sec. He said sure what's up. I asked if he had some coke and the price. He told me yes and the price. The price was fair. We exchanged numbers and he told me to call him the next day. I called him and he told me to meet him with the money. When I met him, I gave him the money, and then he told me where to meet the guy with the coke. I had never done this before and was a little apprehensive. He explained that he never liked to have the coke and the money in the same place at same time. Everything was cool and I was back in action. The only problem dealing with Blow was that he would usually take a few months off. I was not in the position to do the same. I'm not sure how many keys of coke he was getting but I can only assume it was fifty or better. Me and Blow became friends and I don't use that term lightly. We would just sit around and talk about a lot of things. He was a very intelligent individual. He asked me about the girls and how I liked it. I told him it was cool, but also was a headache. We exchanged game and before I knew it Blow had some girls. Game is information or knowledge. I know he really didn't take it seriously. He had way too much going on in his world.

One day when I was leaving my pops gambling house I was in an accident. I remember calling Sunny and telling her. She came with two of the girls I had working for me at the time. I was on a stretcher, but I assured them that I would be ok. I went to the hospital and nothing was broken just bruised up and in pain. Both businesses were doing good and I was recovering from my accident. I finally got my truck out of the shop. Me and an associate named Buddy would go to this gamble house and play craps. Buddy was a pimp but was also a cold-hearted backstabbing individual. I had informed Buddy that I was always packing a gun so we would be ok when were in the gambling house. We had got into a feud one day and had gained mutual respect for one another. One night after we left the gambling house, we both were parked on the track. I was parked several cars behind him. It was about five AM and I had informed my girls that I was about to leave and go eat. They said they had reached their quotas and asked if they could join me. I told them sure and that I would wait for them. As soon as I hung up the phone police came from everywhere. There were about 6 cop cars. The went straight to Buddy's car and pulled him and a couple of his girls out of the car. I slumped down in my seat trying not to be seen. I had TV's installed in my truck and was watching tv. The police came straight to my truck and tapped on the window. I cracked the window and asked if I could help him. He asked me what I was doing, and I told him I was watching TV. He said bullshit, so I rolled the window down so he could see the tv's. He told me to get out of the car and I said for what. He said just get out of the car. I never should have gotten out, but I did. I locked my doors and he said no since of you locking that I'm going in that truck. He searched me and pulled out $1,8000 I had on me. He made a statement, "oh you must be a big pimp." He then took my key, opened my door and began to search my truck. He found my gun and arrested me on the track in front of everybody. My girls had just pulled up when they were putting me in the car. I was not worried at the time, because I did not know that they had changed the law making carrying a pistol without a license a felony now. It was Sunday morning, so I had to stay in jail until that Monday when I went before the judge. I didn't want to use the lawyers I had for my last case. I had used them for the case with Cadillac and they screwed me around. I think they worked with insurance company to have my case dismissed. I was out of the $35,000 cash I paid for the Cadillac. Black had caught a gun charge in Maryland while we were fighting our charge in DC. The lawyer Bobby beat his case, so I went to see Bobby. He told me that he would charge me $10,000 to handle the case and that the case would never see the inside of a court room. Bobby said the radio run was for a man in a white Mercedes with a gun. I was in a green Jeep Cherokee. He also represented a lot of big drug dealers. I paid him the $10,000 and got back to business.

A few weeks later while me and Sunny were riding in my truck this young girl crashed into us. I was beginning to think this truck was a bad omen. It was time to get rid of this truck. Things started to go from bad to worse for me. My gambling had spiraled out of control. I was going to Atlantic city every week and losing tens of thousands of dollars. Then I would gamble home in the city and lose money. I hit a drought and the next thing I knew I was dead broke. I had been broke before, but this time it was different. I had Sunny and her son depending on me. I couldn't believe I had let them down and I fell into a short depression. Sunny was actually out of town and I had advised her of what had happened. I told her I felt horrible that she had put her trust in me, and I had let them down. I told her I understood if she wanted to go separate ways. She told me she would call me back. I actually thought I probably wouldn't hear from her again. The next thing I knew she was walking through the door. She had caught a flight home and this was a big deal because she was terrified of flying. She told me she still believed in me and we were going to get through this. I looked at her and told her she was right. The next day I started calling up all my old connects to see if I could get some coke. I called Jimmy and he told me to meet him so we could talk. I asked him if he had some coke and he told me yes. I told him that I didn't have any money, but I had some cars that were paid for and he could hold the cars and the titles until I paid him his money. He told me that we are family and that would not be necessary. He told me to call him the next day and he would take care of me. I called him for the next couple days, but he never replied. I also had another connect tell me he would give me something on consignment, but he also never returned my calls. Blow would be down on the track from time to time and I happened to run into him. He was always a pleasant guy whenever we saw each other. It seemed like he would light up when he would see me. I asked him if I could talk to him for a second in private. I asked him if he had any coke. He told me he would definitely have some tomorrow. I explained my position to him that I had no money and that I could let him hold my cars and titles. He laughed and said stop playing. We are family. I was like not again. He asked me what I wanted. I had bought anywhere from two to four keys from him at one time in the past. I told him that whatever he could give me would be greatly appreciated. I told him I had not had any coke in a while, and it may take a little time to move it. He told me not to worry and to take my time. He told me to call him the next day. The next day I fully expected my call to go unanswered. To my surprise he called me right back. He told me where to meet the guy. When I pulled up to my surprise it was Blow waiting to meet me. He never had met me with any coke before. That was his thing never to be around the coke. We talked and he told me that we all go through ups and downs, but I was a good dude. We shook hands and went our separate ways. About a month later my pops had informed me that Blow had been arrested by the feds. I was really upset, because I knew he was a good dude. I went to see Blow and he told me this dude had set him up. I told him if I could do anything for him just let me know. I had some money because me and Sunny had just received a small settlement and I had the money I had made off of the last coke I got from Blow.

# Chapter 8

# A Real Hustlers Connect

I couldn't find anyone with any decent prices on coke. Black came to me and told me this dude who smoked crack said he knew some Columbians in New York that had some coke. I laughed and said I'm supposed to put my trust and money in a crackhead. He said what do you have to lose. I said our lives and this little bit of money I got. He told me the crackhead dude use to work for this dude and the Columbians would front him keys of coke. I told him fuck it let's do it. I told him that we go without guns. I told him the guns wouldn't save us if they wanted to rob us but if they thought we were not threatening they probably wouldn't kill us. I don't think I told my pops, because I know he would have been highly against this. I rented a limo and all three of us took the trip to New York. We had the limo driver park in downtown Manhattan. We caught a cab uptown. We met with a Columbian named Kito. When we first met, he asked me did I know the guy he use to front keys to, because the guy had ran off with his money. I told him I didn't know the guy. I told him I didn't want anything on consignment. I was willing to pay for whatever I got. I just wanted it to be quality. I didn't have enough to get a whole key, so I got a half and a quarter which they charged more because they had to open it. We caught a cab back to the limo and went home. Black asked me, why did I rent the limo. I told him once we were inside the limo on the highway there would be no reason for the police to pull us over. They wouldn't know who is inside this limo unless someone was to ever snitch. I told him never tell anyone about the route and this would be the last time the crackhead could go. The coke from Kito was good and sold fast. I was back in New York in four days. I had enough for the whole key this time, but Kito told me he couldn't get me any good coke. I appreciated him not selling me some bad coke. I left and had my limo driver stop in Atlantic city. I proceeded to lose $7,000. I went in the bathroom and looked in the mirror. I told myself I could not let my gambling addiction destroy me again. This was the first time in my life that I was able to walk away losing and have money in my pocket. It generally was win big or lose it all. A few days later Kito called me and told me to come back up. I didn't have enough for a key again because of my trip to Atlantic city. After that trip I was able to buy a whole key. I was going to New York once a week. I figured I needed to find another limo company so that it would not be obvious to the company what I was doing. An associate told me he knew a couple who had a limo service. I didn't' tell him what for and of course not them. They would charge me $1,000 for the day. I told them I was in the music business and really didn't like to fly. They would pick me up around 6 am and we would get to New York in about three and half hours depending on traffic. The driver Gerry was an older black man that had a heavy foot on the wheel. I would generally stay up all night so I could sleep on the way up. On one particular trip I remember I woke up and saw sirens behind us. At first, I was scared, but I only had money on me. When we pulled off. I asked Gerry what happened. He told me he got pulled over for speeding. I told him to take it easy and I would pay for his ticket. The other limo company was a place where I used to get my car washed. The driver Bill was an older white man and he was really cool. Sunny asked could she ride up with me one time so she could do some shopping. I told her sure. I remember us fucking in the back of the limo. Another time I took one of my other girls at the time up with me. This was one of those days where it seemed it took Kito forever to get the coke. I left her in the car and Bill told her that his partner thought I was into something more than music. Bill told her he defended me and told his partner to mind his fucking business. I was a little nervous, but I continued to use both services. I never allowed any of my girls to ride up with me anymore except on one occasion when I was going to buy me a mink coat. I wanted Sunny's opinion on the coat. The next thing I knew Sunny wanted a coat as well. The coat I was looking at was $10,000. They actually wanted to design her a coat that would have cost around $15,000. I only had ten thousand over what I had brought to buy the coke. I told them to start working on her coat and I would buy both coats at the same time. On the drive home she told me she didn't want me to spend that much on a coat. She would just pick something off of the rack. I called and canceled the order. It was a good thing that I didn't get the coats at that time. Later on, I went back in the store and I met the owner.

We hit it off. The coat I was going to pay ten thousand for he sold it to me for $6,000. I brought Sunny a coat that cost $7,000. So, I basically saved $11,000 just because the owner liked me. Sunny talked me into buying two mink hats. One was a baseball cap made out of mink and the other was a cowboy hat that I paid $500 for and never wore. I remember getting that coat I thought I was a super star. My pops had convinced me a while ago that I could not go around dressed like my peers. I was deep in the dope game, but I didn't want to look like your typical dopeboy. He told me to get rid of all my dungarees. I had no idea what dungarees were and he could tell by the look on my face I had no clue what he was talking about. He said you call them jeans. It brought me back to a memory when he made me buy my first pair of Bally dress shoes. They were $200 and I was pissed because I didn't want to pay two hundred dollars for shoes I was not going to wear. I changed my entire wardrobe just as my pops had instructed me to do. I brought some of the finest suits by Versace, Brioni, Armani and more. I brought Mauri shoes that cost anywhere from $600 to $1,100. Most days I was in a suit and tie or at least slacks and a collared shirt. One day I was in the barber shop I had on one of my finest suits with matching Mauri shoes. One of the local guys wanted to be funny and asked me if I was going to a funeral because I was dressed in a suit. He got a few laughs. I told him this is what people with money dress like and I'm sure you wouldn't understand. I got even more laughs. He was like dam I was only joking with you. I looked at him and told him I wasn't. I was always the type of individual that was laid back and usually chill, but don't try to play me or be disrespectful. That would never be tolerated. By this time, I was carrying around four or five thousand dollars on me at any given time. I remember one day I had just left the barbershop and the barbershop which also had a salon connected to it got robbed. I felt that I could have been in there at the time. I was pissed because me and the owner Roy were cool. He had no idea who had done it. I felt like I could have been one of the targets, but couldn't prove it and I was not there so I just made sure I didn't have that type of money on me unless I had Tank or someone with me sitting in the shop that was strapped with a gun. I was tired of the demon green Cherokee. I had two accidents locked up in this vehicle. I told my sister Ann I wanted to get a new car. She told me the only way she would sign is if I brought something with a car note. I could not pay cash for it. I went to the Jeep dealership just to look. They had this new Jeep with vents in the hood. I thought it looked so cool. I explained to the salesman that I wanted to trade my truck in for the newer model. He asked me how much I wanted for my truck because it was paid for. I told him fourteen thousand. I also told him I would be bringing my sister to sign for the truck and if we could have all the paper ready to go it would be appreciated because she would be just getting off work. He agreed and the next day me and Ann went to the dealership. She had just worked a double and was extremely tired. They had all the paperwork ready except they were telling me I had to pay this destination charge of five hundred dollars twice. I explained to them that it didn't make since for them to add a five hundred destination charge onto the truck when it is already included in the price of the truck. It was an older salesman working with the younger salesman and told me it didn't work like that. I told him I could read, add and count. The destination charge was clearly included in the price and there was no way I was going to pay for it twice. It was only five hundred dollars, but it was the principle that he was trying to play me for a fool. I got pissed and told Ann let's leave and we did. I called around to all the Jeep dealers in the area. Most of them did not have the truck yet because it was scheduled to be released to most dealers in a few months. A few dealers had made orders as if they had a customer that had preordered the truck. The guys who were giving me the run around were the only dealership who had a cobalt black truck. A few dealers had the platinum silver one, but I was in love with the cobalt black. I swallowed my pride and called the guys with the cobalt jeep truck only to find out they sold it. They told me they had a platinum one. I decided to go to another dealership and get it. The truck was so new and rare at the time the sales manager wrote on the paperwork. No deals, full price or don't sell the truck. I had already saved five hundred dollars and I was willing to pay for the truck, because I wanted it. A few weeks after I got my truck, I was getting out and this dude said to me I see you got your truck. I looked at him with a puzzled look. He explained he was one of the salesmen that was trying to sell me the cobalt colored jeep. He told me the issue was that they were not trying to give me the fourteen thousand I wanted for my truck. They only wanted to give me thirteen thousand five hundred. He told the older salesman just be

80

honest, but he came up with that stupid plan. I said yes, he cost you a commission and me my cobalt jeep, but I was happy with the platinum.

I heard there was this club in Nashville Tennessee that girls where getting money. I only had two girls at the time Sunny and another girl. I decided to take a trip. Before I left me, and Black had a heart to heart talk. He told me that him and BB had been talking. He said BB said I should be giving them a better price. I was a little pissed and hurt. I gave both of them the opportunity to be my partners. I told him that I have to go get the stuff take a risk of that. Then I have to take a risk if the stuff is not good, then I give it you both and have to wait for you to sell it and then get my money. You don't think I deserve to make a profit? I told him I love you like a brother, but business is business. I told him if he puts his own money up. He could put his money with mine and get it for the same price, but BB would have to still pay the price I'm charging. After our talk I got on the road. I loved Black and always wanted to see him shine, but I felt like he might allow BB to poison our relationship. When we were younger somehow BB got us all to gamble and we were trying to win each other's money. My pops despised BB and told me he didn't trust him. He thought BB would be a snitch. He found out we all were gambling, and he told me that it was no good for me and Black to be gambling. My pops asked me would I gamble and try to win his money. I told him absolutely not. He said Black is family and we should never try to win each other's money. It was about an eight-hour ride and I had time to think about a lot. Once we got there Sunny and the other girl went to work in the club. That next day Black called me and asked me when I would be back. I told him things were not as good as I was told, and I would be back probably tomorrow. We would be back in action Monday. I knew BB was searching for cheaper prices. My pops always told me if you got a good reliable connect you can trust, stick with them. Even if the prices are a little higher. Stay with them, because it's hard to find people to trust in this game. I told Black whatever he did not to trust BB. I got back that Sunday night and I was chilling with my cousin Fats. My pops paged me and put code 911 in. That was a code for emergency and my pops knew nothing about this code. I freaked out and called him immediately. He Told me something had happened and Black and BB was at his house. I got all my money together and gave it to Sunny. I told her to go and get a hotel room and wait for my call. I had no idea what was going on. I raced over to my pops house. When I got their Black and BB told me that had tried to make a drug deal and it went bad. I was shocked and taken aback. I told them I didn't want to know the details. All I knew is that whatever happened, happened. They asked what I think they should do. I told them they needed to go and talk to a lawyer. He wanted to go and see Bobby. I had told him to be careful because I felt like Bobby was fucking up on my case. They told Bobby what had transpired. The guy had actually tried to rob them, and shots were fired. Black or BB were not hit but the dude was. They didn't know his condition, but he later died. Bobby agreed to take the case I believe for twenty-five thousand. He would be representing Black, because I guess he was going to be the fall guy in this situation. BB was trying to stay far and clear from the scene, although he was the one who set the meeting up with the dude. He was trying to get some coke for a cheaper price and drug Black into his bullshit. Before we left Black told Bobby don't fuck up, because I told him he was fucking up on my case. I was pissed with Black, because Bobby was still representing in my case. Not a good job though. We all left. I called Sunny and told her she could go back to the house. BB and Black both got locked up. BB called me and told me he could get a bond, but he needed ten thousand dollars. He asked me if he could borrow it until he got out. I told him sure. I didn't really understand how he got could get a bond and Black could not. The next day he called me from his sister's house and informed me he was out, but still needed the ten thousand dollars. It sounded strange to me. I told him I would give him a call back and immediately went and changed all my numbers. I didn't know what he was up to, but I knew he was up to no good. A few days later my cell rang, and it was Black. He began to scream in the phone that nigga snitching. At that moment my house phone rang, and it was lawyer. He said have you talk to your cousin. I said yes, he's on the other phone. He Said BB was snitching. I told Bobby I knew and that I would talk to him later. I got back on the phone with Black and told him that BB was a bitch and somehow, he would get his. I was furious, Black was like my brother and he had gotten caught up in BB's bullshit and then he has the audacity to snitch. I was still dealing with my gun case at the time and it was

82

apparent the judge did not like me or my lawyer. That day we went to court and the judge instructed the prosecutor and Bobby my lawyer to go to the court of appeals and find cases that best supported their arguments. He gave them both 2 hours. Bobby came back with several cases that sited illegal search and seizure. The prosecution had absolutely nothing. The judge stated that it seemed like a close decision, but he would let it go forth and allow a jury to hear the case. I thought how could it be close, when they didn't follow your instructions. He asked the prosecutor was he going to use the eighteen hundred dollars the police found on me the night I was arrested. He told the judge since there was no drugs found he wouldn't be using that as evidence. The judge told him that the money could only help his case. I whispered to my lawyer is he going to be part of the prosecution too. He scheduled the trial to start immediately. The next day they brought in potential jurors. I saw this dude that went to school with me. I told my lawyer that I knew someone on the jury. We had attended the same high school together. My lawyer asked was he a friend or foe. I told him we were pretty cool in school. In the beginning he acted as if he didn't know me. The judge asked did the jurors if they knew me, my lawyer or the prosecutor. He asked twice, and then he asked for a third time and this bitch stood up and told them he knew me and of course you know they dismissed his ass. I was pissed until Sunny told me one of the jurors told her I had nothing to worry about. I went to my pops and asked should I offer the juror a few dollars. He told me that was a stupid idea. He said you have a bullshit gun case, but if you mess with a juror that's a federal crime. Bobby was completely unprepared for this case. The prosecution kept talking about the eighteen hundred dollars I had. They said I had the gun to protect the eighteen hundred dollars. My rebuttal was that I had the money to pay taxes on a property me and my pops owned, but when I took the stand Bobby never asked me about the money. The trial ended on Thursday evening and the jury started deliberating. I remember waking up that Friday morning. I put on one of my best suits and some black Mauri gator shoes. I went to meet Bobby to ask him what he thought. He told me that he felt confident with the case and the worse he saw me getting was probation. I told him I didn't give you ten thousand dollars to get probation on this bullshit case. He said that was the absolutely worse case scenario. We left to go to court. We were not there long when the jury reached a verdict. The juror who said I had nothing to worry about came out looked at me and shook his and then looked down, I knew I had been found guilty. I tapped Bobby and said we had loss this one. He looked at me and said what are you talking about.

# Chapter 9

# Hustler Found Guilty

The verdict was in, guilty! I heard Ann and Sunny scream and start crying. I looked at them and told them to be cool. Bobby asked for me to be allowed to remain on bond and stated this case had taken almost two years and I had not got in anymore trouble. The Judge denied his motion and told the bailiff to take me away. When they put me in a holding cell behind the court. A young dude made a comment, "Oh shit they are locking up lawyers." I looked at the dude and told him I was not in the mood for joke and games. He said my bad and I sat down furious with what had just taken place. They transferred me to DC Jail while I was awaiting to be sentenced. Once I got there, I had to go through intake. They take all your clothes and your shoestrings. They ask you are you thinking about hurting anyone or hurting yourself. I replied no to both. I got an orange jumper. What a site. I was in an orange jumper in my $600 Mauris shoes. I met an older guy named Wes who seemed cool. I think he liked to get high and party with powder. He was in there on some type of credit card fraud which was a federal crime I believe.

The food and everything about this place was inhumane. I was in a cell with this young dude who knew some of my younger cousins. The only thing I could really eat at the time was fruit. Some of the stuff I couldn't even tell you what it was. I made a deal with my cellmate. I told him he could have all of my food trays if he gave me his fruit. He agreed and everything was cool. Until one day I went on a visit to see my pops. When I came back from my visit it was a strong smell of oranges in our cell. I looked and he ate his orange as well as my orange. At that moment they popped my cell and told me I had a visit. It was my pops again. This jail was so stupid and backwards. You got an hour visit per day, but it had to be split up in two half hour visits. So even if the same person was coming for both half hour visits, they had to go downstairs after the first half hour. Sign in again and then come back up. My pops immediately asked what was wrong with me. I informed him the dude had ate my orange and when I went back to my cell, I was going to beat his ass. He looked at me with a stern looked and asked if I was crazy. He reminded me that I had just a gun charge with no priors. The opportunity for me to get probation and come home looked good. As long as I didn't do anything to get into any more trouble. As usual he was right and I was blessed he was the one coming to see me, because I probably would have not listened to anyone else. I went back to my cell and I told my cellmate not to touch anything on my tray ever again or I was going to beat his ass. Every meal I would just take off the fruit and leave the rest. One day the guy passing out the food asked me if I wanted to give my food to my cellmate. I told him no, throw that shit in the trash he can't have it. I finally got moved to the sentencing block and boy was I happy. I could finally start to get canteen. Canteen was the store in jail that sold personal items, food and sodas. When I first got to the block. I walked in and this guy that was about six five and three hundred pounds asked me if I was in cell sixty-seven. When I said yes, he was like yes and seemed very happy. I really didn't know how to take his reaction. I know that I was not down with no homosexual shit. I thought I'll just take these shoes and kick him in the face from the top bunk. He came into the cell and introduced himself. He said his name was Shotty and that he was happy they had put another young dude in the cell with him. He told me the last dude was old, dirty and nasty. He said we both had to live here for the time being and it was up to us to keep it as clean as possible. I told him cool and we shook hands. That day they passed out canteen. I was unable to get any because it had already been ordered before I got to the block. Shotty had a big bag of stuff. He told me I could help myself to anything in his bag just let him know so he wouldn't think someone stole something. I told him cool, but I had no intentions on taking anything from this dude. It was a Friday and they said they were going to be passing out ice. They had canned sodas, but they didn't always have ice so you either drunk hot sodas or waited for days they passed out ice. Shotty said we would drink some cold sodas, eat chips, play checkers and talk. I was not interested. The night came he took out the checkers board and offered me a soda. I told him no I was cool. He looked at me and said, "look celly I don't want nothing from you, I know your ass thirsty and tired of drinking that water and that nasty ass juice." I told him he was right and took the soda. It had been three weeks since I had anything but water and this nasty jail juice. That coke soda tasted like cold champagne. He told me about where he was from and a little about his case. I told him a little about me and my case. He was facing twenty-five to life for attempted murder. He was a murderer, robber guy in the streets. I told him I didn't justify his hustle on the street, but I understood. I told him I was a hustler and had some girls that worked for me. We became pretty cool.

One day him and his crew were sharpening a shank in our cell. Shotty told them they had to go to another cell because I had a chance of going home. The old guy Wes was moved into our block and he was in my cell and we were talking one day. He saw my money receipt laying on the table. He said is that your money receipt and I replied yes. He said that I should hide it because if guys knew I had a thousand dollars in my account they might try to extort me. I laughed and told Wes I'm not no dude that runs around and pretends to be tough, but there is no way no one would ever extort me. Canteen came and I ordered so much they denied some stuff. I noticed Shotty didn't get anything this time. I told him that he was welcome to anything in my bag. Just let me know. He said he didn't want me to feel because he gave me something that I had to do the same. I told him that he didn't know anything about me when I walked in the door and didn't know if I would ever be able to buy canteen. I told him I'm doing it because he was cool with me. It was a stressful time for me to say the least. Bobby had told me even if I got found guilty. I would never do one day in jail. Now I was looking at up to 10 years, because they classified my gun as a machine gun because it shot more than 10 times.

Me and Sunny were ok, but I had another one of my girls I had started to become very close with. Her name was Ivy. Ivy a was hard worker and we had what I thought was an amazing bond and chemistry. I was about to get her a town house and a car. My pops and sister were upset with me because I had left all my money with Sunny. It was not my intentions, but everything happened so fast and the money was at my house in the attic. I just told her to take it and put it in a safety deposit box. They screwed up my paperwork so when I went to get sentenced, they couldn't sentence me. I had to wait another forty days to see the judge and I was pissed. My business was falling apart while I was gone. Ivy had wound up leaving because she didn't know how much time I was going to get. My pops came to visit me and told me he needed some money. He told me he didn't want to burden me, but he needed it. I asked him how much he needed, and he told me five thousand dollars. I told him fine Sunny would bring him the money the next day. She was holding a $130,000 of my money. I told her it was a guy at the barbershop that owed me five thousand. I told her to get that and give it to my pops. When I called home, she told me he had only given her half the money and would have the rest in two days. I said fine give that to my pops and explain he'll have the rest in two days. Later that night I called, and she told me my pops had thrown the money in her face and said if I couldn't afford or want to give it to him, I should have said so. She said she tried to explain but he was just yelling at her, so she left. I called my pops and he is yelling and screaming in the phone. I let him finish and asked if I could talk. He said go ahead. I explained that I had told her to get the five thousand form this dude that owed me money, instead of running back to the safety deposit box. The dude would have the other half in two days, and she would give you the rest then. He said he didn't know she was saying that, and he could wait two days for the rest. He apologized, and I told him no worries. He thought she might not want to give him the money. I told him she was a good woman and did what I said to do. He got his money and even apologized to Sunny. I was shocked. The sentencing block was a revolving door for the most part. New dudes coming in and other dudes getting shipped out after their sentencing. A whole crew came in on a big drug and murder case. I was pretty cool with the dudes at the top of the case. They basically came in and took over the block phones and TV's. They told me I had access to the phones whenever I wanted. A few people knew me from the streets from getting money, so I really never had any problems. I had extra lines installed in my house so I could call home more. Sunny would basically call my friends and associates on three way. We generally got 10 minutes on the phone and then you let the next person in line use the phone. Usually in the morning there where never lines to use the phones. One day I had been on the phone over an hour and this guy walks up and says, "I told you niggas about being on the phone all day." I told Tank to hold on because he was walking towards me. He stopped short of me and hung the guy's phone up next to me. They had words and the guy who was on the phone backed down. I was waiting on him to hang my phone up so I could hit him in the head with the receiver. He looked at me and didn't say anything and just walked away. I told Tank what had happened. He asked what I would have done if he hung my phone up. I told him you would have heard the receiver busting his head open. He told me I have to be cool so I could come home. I explained I have to live in here until I come home and if I let him hang up my phone, next he will take my canteen and so on. The guy who hung the phone up must have said something to Shotty. Shotty asked was my pops and girls ok? I said yes why. He said he didn't want to get into it with a dude about a phone. I told him that I'm always respectful if people are waiting. I told him fuck that dude if he had a problem with me tell him to say it to my face.

Me and Sunny were supposed to take our little man to Disney world and I felt horrible. I told her to take the whole family and have a good time. I didn't know how expensive Disney world was. Ivy was supposed to come and see me one day, but she never showed. She was not sure how much time I was going to get and was unwilling to stand by my side. I was glad I found out before I got her the house and the new car. The sentencing block was crazy and tense. Dudes would go to court and come back with ninety years. Here I am probably going to get probation. I kept my head low, but never went for no bullshit. I spent a lot of time learning to play chess. I had started to do two for ones. At the time you could still buy cigarettes which was more powerful than money. Me and Shotty would give a guy one cigarette and on canteen day he would repay us with two. I told my pops and once again he was the voice of reason. He said you got money right. I replied yes. He said what are you going to do if someone does not pay you. He said I already know what you're going to do. He told me to leave it alone and start being smarter with my decision making. I told Shotty he could do the two for one. Just give me my one back and he could keep the extra one. On the next canteen day he was sharpening a shank. I asked what was up and he told me the dude had not paid his debt. I told him to give the dude a pass, but he was not having it. He said the dude had to pay, in cigarettes, in blood or move out the block. The guy got transferred out of the block. My sentencing day was here. It was Friday morning. The judge sentenced me to three years' probation, a five thousand dollar fine and he banned me from DC. My pops stood up and stated he lived in DC. The judge said I could be in DC between nine am to five pm and then I had to be gone. I was just happy to know I was going home. Once again, they screwed up my paperwork and I was told I would not be released until Monday. That night about 1AM they popped my cell and called my name. They told me I had less than twenty minutes to get my stuff or I would have to wait until Monday to leave. I left everything. They let me out about 2AM with no money, in some camouflage pants and a white tee shirt. I made a collect call to Ann and she came and picked me up. I was so happy to be out and now once again it was time to get back to business.

# Chapter 10

# A Hustlers Comeback

I felt I needed a little vacation. I went to Las Vegas with Sunny and one of my best friends Cubano and his girl. We had a ball but as usual I got broke gambling. I took Sunny shopping first. She wanted some shoes and purse that cost a thousand dollars. Once I got broke she asked me if I wanted her to go to work. I told her we were on vacation and to relax. I told her I would get some money wired from an associate. Cubano was broke as well, I asked him if he had anyone that would send him some money. He said the friend that would send him some money was out Vegas broke with him. I split my money with him. I loss that too and it was our last day. Sunny was playing the slots and asked me to sit with her. She hit for a thousand dollars. I told her to go and get her bag and shoes. She gave me the money and told me go win us some money. I loss that too. Once I got back, I went to meet Kito. He told me he didn't have anything, but he knew some Dominicans that had some, but we had to go to get it. I had developed a lot of trust in Kito so I agreed. We went to the Bronx. I was waiting in this phone store in the back office. This guy comes in and says hey whats up. I just said whats up. He asked me how much my guy was charging me. I told him I had no idea what he was talking about. He explained he was the man and that Kito was with one of his workers. He told me if I like the coke take his number and give him a call, because he could beat my guy's price. I took the number. I started to deal with Greg when his prices were better than Kito. I would usually buy four keys of coke and he sometimes could beat Kito's price by two thousand per kilo. That's a savings of eight to ten thousand. I was only selling strictly powder. I would only add three to four thousand on each kilo. I was making twelve to sixteen thousand a week. Everyone I dealt with was eating good. I would front you whatever you wanted as long as you could have my money in three days. I took on a new associate named Pat, whom I had known since I was a kid. We went to the same elementary school. Pat used to deal with Black before Black went away to jail. Pat was a good dude, but a little bit egotistical. When he got drunk a little bit of an asshole. I had put him on, and he was getting money. We began to grow a close bond. Sunny warned me against him, but I didn't heed her warning. We had moved our son down here. We had moved into the house in Maryland that me and my pops now owned. I had him going to a private school. I had finally broken the $200,000 barrier and I wanted a son of my own. The game with the girls was cool but, I was tired of the bullshit and the money was not close to the same.

I told Sunny she had been with me going on four years let's have a baby of our own. I told her to stop working and go to school to be a nurse. She was doing amazing in school and me and her mom were so proud of her. She was getting all A's. Then the day came when her and the teacher got into it and she lost her cool. Sunny sat in the back of the class by herself when school had first started. She began to make friends and I assume they began to sit in the back with her. The teacher asked her to move to the front of the class. Sunny refused and they got into some type of verbal altercation and Sunny was suspended. She never went back to school after that. I told her that she had allowed that lady to stop her from becoming successful. The lady already had her nursing certification. I told her she had to be smarter than that. She began to hang out with some local girls she had met at the club. I told her I did not trust those girls and didn't want them in my house. One day I was leaving and one of the girls pulled up to my house. She knocked on my door and Sunny let her in. I went back in the house and asked her had she lost her mind. She told me if I didn't like her friend for me to tell her to leave. I walked out into my living room where the girl was sitting and told her to get out of my house and never come back. I told Sunny I can't control whom you're with when you leave this house, but I will control who comes in and out of this house. Everything was going pretty good. We had just moved into the house and the lease on the place in VA was about to be up. One night I was going to get some clothes and decided not to. Instead me and my cousin Fats went out to a strip club. Later that night when I got home, I saw yellow police tape four houses down from mine. When I went in the house my mom and Sunny were watching tv. I asked them did they hear anything and they both told me no. Sunny said the police had knocked on

92

the door and asked them if they heard anything and she told them no also. A couple days later I found out my nephew had been locked up for murder. Now let me give you a little backdrop on my nephew. Him and his mom had moved into the house and I paid all the bills for him and then his sister moved in. He became very disrespectful to my pops and his mom. We had gotten into several verbal and one physical altercation. The physical altercation happened one day when I came into the house and he was yelling at my pops. That's a definite no no. I jumped on him and told him that would not be accepted. He later dropped out of school and came to me and told me he wanted to hustle. I told him I had no problems with giving him some work, but he would have to get the ok from his mom and my pops. He did and I began to front him work. The problem is he would never pay me. He always had an excuse to why he couldn't pay me or how he messed up the money. He also got shot in the neck and I asked him what happened so that I could handle it for him. He lied and told me didn't know who or why he got shot. I told him fine. I also told him that if he didn't pay me this time. I could no longer do business with him. I explained I had to pay for the product, and I was charging him the same price, I was getting it for. Of course, he didn't pay me, and we stopped doing business. I asked my pops what was going on with my nephew's case? He immediately came to me and said the detective was talking crazy. He asked my pops how close was his son and grandson? He said that we were ok. He said from their initial investigation it seemed like your grandson was trying to rob your son. A couple days had gone by and I had found out that my nephew's friend whom he used to be with every day was the one was killed on my street. It all started to make sense what the detective was saying. I was enraged. I asked my pops did he have a bond. My pops told me not to be silly. You are not going to bond him out. I knew if they were going to come and rob me that they were also going to kill me. My pops told me not to go to court because he didn't want the detectives to see me and start to wonder why they were looking to rob this young guy. Two dudes who were with them testified against my nephew. They said they were waiting on me to come home. When I didn't show one of the dudes said you don't know when you uncle is coming home. If we keep standing on the side of this house someone may call the cops. They began to walk down the street and argue. My nephew said the dude had messed his chance up to get this money. My nephew pulled out the gun and said I should kill you. The dude said fuck you and my nephew shot him twice in the head. This caused a divide between some of our family members including me and my pops. My pops had told me he would always have my back no matter what, unless he found out I was robbing people. I was upset he continued to go to talk to the lawyer with my sister Sonya, but I understood a little. At a family reunion, a few of my cousins were talking about how it was messed he was in jail. My nephew tried to convince our family that the dude was coming to rob me, and he killed him because of it. I asked them if they knew that someone was going to do something to me, what would be the first thing they would do? They all said call me. So why didn't he. I told him the reason he didn't, because he was the master mind behind the scheme. After my nephew had been convicted, my pops and I stopped speaking, because I found out he went to see him. I was angry, hurt and felt betrayed. A mutual friend of ours Whitefolks, called me to his store to talk to me and try to smooth things out between me and my pops. He explained that he loved his daughter and only went to the lawyer with her because he didn't want a lawyer to try and take advantage of her. I told him that was fine, but I found out my pops went to visit my nephew. He said my pops was wrong and he didn't know that. He also told me how much my father loved me, and it was nothing he wouldn't do for me and we needed to talk. I called my pops and went to see him. He told me he was wrong for going to see him and promised me he wouldn't go see him again. After we got through that ordeal. The next thing I knew, someone else had talked about trying to kidnap and rob me. My pops had come to me with a name and asked me did I know this dude. I told him no, and I quickly went to my crew and told them that if they found out who this dude was it would be a reward for them. My pops found out who it was and went to the dudes. He told them if anything happened to me, he would have them killed. They told him they were not looking to get me, but another dude. My pops told me this and I was livid with him once again. I told him they would not confess to him that they wanted me because they know the consequences. I begged him to tell me who these guys were, but he wouldn't. He just said he handled it. I found out later the reason why he protected these dudes is that one of

94

them was one his ex-girlfriend's son. I knew the dude and he was a cold coward. He must have had some other dude try to put that in his head.

Then after that out of nowhere a drought hit and I couldn't get any coke from any of my connects. Pat told me he had some dudes in Chicago that had some coke, but not sure if they would be willing to deal with me. The dude was originally from our neighborhood, but he had moved to Chicago. I told Pat to go talk to him and tell him I had $100,000 cash I was willing to spend. He reluctantly agreed to do business with me. I rented a van and had Sunny ride out with me. Once I got there and met with him. We both knew each other. It had been a long time since we had seen each other, but we hugged and laughed. His name was Dre. He said I remember when you were little playing football. I watched you grow up. I asked how he had been. He said good, he was just hesitant to deal with anybody from the old neighborhood because most of them was on bullshit. I got four keys of cocaine from him. Nobody in the city basically had any coke and if they did, they were only selling ounces. I got back and made sure my crew was straight. A few of my crew complained about the prices. Dudes were trying to sell keys of coke for forty thousand. I only charged thirty-five thousand. I told them if they could find something of similar quality at a cheaper price, and if it was not of good quality could they get their money back with no questions asked. They should do it. I explained to them about good business decisions and how I always looked out for them. They agreed and paid my price. A few days later I was on my way back to Chicago. I made forty thousand off of the first trip. The second trip was all together crazy. On my way back I got side swiped by a car and the car just sped off. I began to chase the car until I came to my senses and realized that if I got pulled over, I was getting more than just a ticket. Pat had bought some coke as well. His package was short and so was mine. That was my last trip to Chicago. I still was one of the only dudes to have coke in the city. My old connect Jimmy came up to the barbershop where I got my haircut. I thought it was odd. He asked if I had some coke and I told him yes. He said he had run into my cousin Fats and he told him I didn't fuck with him. I told him that when I came to him and needed a favor, he told me he would do it and then vanished. He told me somethings transpired and he couldn't. I told him

95

that was fine, but don't treat me like some hoe and not return my calls. He told me him and his cousin Kev both needed some coke, but they didn't have any money. I knew that was bullshit, but I told them I could front them whatever they wanted, I just needed my money in three days. They agreed and I gave them the coke. When Kev came to pay me. I pulled out my money counter I had gotten from my Dominican connect Greg. He laughed and said, "who do you think you are Scarface?" I laughed and explained that I had a dude try to give me some counterfeit bills. I used it when counting large sums of money for accuracy and make sure all money is real. I met Jimmy later that day and collected the twenty thousand he owed me. I thought to myself how the tables had turned. I was proud of myself for not letting emotions get in the way of business. I mean the stuff was going to sell and I didn't have to front them anything. Later that week I did one of the dumbest things I had ever done. I was going to meet an associate with a half of key of cocaine on my lap. I was running late which was something my pops told me to never do. You always get to the meeting spot early so you can check it out. I missed my turn and I went down this street I knew they had speed traps. I was till speeding when I saw the police. He told me to pull over and I did. I was cool, calm and collected. I was sitting there with a half of key of powder on my lap. I grabbed all my paperwork out of my glove compartment and placed it on my lap covering the coke. I got my license and registration out. The officer asked did I know why he pulled me over. I said yes sir, I was speeding. I knew if he asked me to step out of the car I was about to speed off. He came back to the truck and told me he appreciated my honesty, slow down and have a nice day.

Things were going from bad to worse with me and Sunny. The shit really hit the fan once we found out she couldn't get pregnant. We went to a fertility specialist and they told her that it was a 90 something percent she could not have kids. She was devastated and crushed. I told her don't worry about it. I would just adopt our son and continue to raise him as mine. She went into depression and started drinking. Our relationship got combative to say the least. I was on probation and couldn't stand any bullshit charges especially a domestic. One night me and my cousin Fats was leaving the gambling house when he alerted me someone was in my truck. I hit the lights and it was Sunny. She was drunk and smelled like a brewery. Fats asked if I wanted him to go home and try and keep the peace. I told him I got it and dropped him off. After I dropped him off Sunny became irate in the back seat. She actually hit me. I told her if she hit me again, I was going to beat her ass and she was going to the hospital. I knew that we couldn't continue you to do this. Once we got home, I told Sunny that I was done. I told her that I would get her a place and pay for it for a year. I would furnish the place and even give her some money. This made her even more irate. I was in the guest bedroom and she was in the master bedroom. Our son thankfully was at the babysitter. She went and got one of my guns. She asked me if I wanted to be with her. I didn't know she had the gun. I told her no I was done. She told me that if she couldn't have me then no woman could, and she shot at me. I was shocked and pissed at the same time. I immediately jumped up and went towards her. She was so drunk and told me to come on. I caught myself because I knew she was drunk out of her mind. I went to walk out the door and she fired another shot. I had left the house with no keys to the car or truck. I called Fats and told him to come and get me. He pulled up and asked if I wanted him to go and talk to her. I told him she doesn't even like your ass she might kill you. I waited for a while to make sure none of my neighbors called the police. I told Fats to leave I would be alright. I knocked on the door and she came to the door a little sober and said what. I told her to open my dam door. She opened the door and I went and laid on the couch in the living room. She came in and asked was I coming to bed. I told her go lay down before I kill her ass. I was still pissed. I never had a dude in the streets shoot at me. The next day we talked, and I told her what she had done. She was so drunk she could barely remember anything. I told her I loved and cared about her, but this relationship had become too toxic for us both. I got her a place, furnished it and gave her some money just in case something happened to me. I talked to her mom and she agreed the best thing for our son was for him to move back to Milwaukee until Sunny got herself together, so that's what we did. I wanted him to stay with me, but they were not going for that. Money was really flowing, and me and my pops had become so close. We were more like big brother and little brother. He kept telling me that I had to get a business to get out of the life. I told him I was looking into several business ventures but had not found the right one yet. I thought about getting back into the music business. At one time when I was not making any money I had made some rap tapes. My cousin Tank had set me up with some studio time and I had made some demos. Once I started to make money again and was in New York, I saw this rapper that was pretty popular get off the bus. I quickly lost interest in rapping. I knew I had to do something, but I had no idea of what. I was out eating lunch at a deli my mom used to take us to. Three ladies walked in and I couldn't keep my eyes off the Spanish lady with them. She looked at me and smiled and I knew I had her. I offered to pay for all of their lunches. They all thanked me and told me they would take me out to lunch the next time. I asked for the Spanish lady's number. She said you don't even know my name. I told her that I'm sure you are going to put it on the paper beside your number. She laughed and put both on the paper. Her name was Sandy. I called a few days later and asked if I could take her to lunch. She asked if her co-workers could come and I said sure. We went to this Chinese restaurant. We were all laughing and having a good time. Sandy asked me what I did for a living. I was a little caught off guard, but I used my answer I always used when people would ask me. I have a dump truck business. She told me after lunch her two co-workers who were Black scolded her for embarrassing me. They told her I didn't own any dump trucks. They said that boy is a drug dealer. They said he seems like a nice young man, but don't be so naïve. She didn't believe them at first. They told her he is free anytime of the day and carries around big stacks of money. On our second date she flat out asked me was I a drug dealer. I laughed and asked her what made her think that. She told me the story. I told her I was a businessman and I would have to leave it at that. She was cool with it. She told me she was married, but she was separated. They still lived in the same house, which I thought was weird. We had been dating a couple weeks when she told me he wanted the house to himself that weekend, because his girlfriend was coming into town from Florida. She asked if she could stay at my place. I asked her if she wanted to go to Miami for a few days and she said sure. I went to see my travel agent and she said for what it's going to cost me to go to Miami I could go to Cancun Mexico. I called her and asked if she wanted to go to Mexico instead and of course she said yes. Sandy was

98

different from a lot females I had dealt with. First, she was Chilean. Her father worked at the embassy or something important. One day I told her I use to have girls. She was shocked and couldn't believe it. She said you're such a nice gentleman and I couldn't believe you did that. I told her I'm still a nice gentleman that just had a business opportunity and took it. She told me she had a secret and before she could tell me. I said you use to be an escort. She looked at me and said how do you know. I told her I can just tell. She explained she had gotten into a lot of debt in college and didn't want her dad to know. We both laughed and I said I wish I knew her then. She smiled and said you would have taken all my money. I told her I have never taken anyone's money. She said I would have given you all my money and I said yes, because there is a difference. A few days before our trip I called and asked if she wanted to go shopping. She declined and I couldn't believe it. She told me she could take herself to get what she needed. This made me really like her even more. We drove to the airport and when we were getting out of the car. She asked if I was leaving my jewelry in the car. I told her no. She said baby we are going to a third world country and they will cut your hand off for it. I put the jewelry in the car. We had to catch a bus from the airport to the hotel. It was pretty dark on the bus and I saw something running back and forth on the seat. It was the biggest bug I had ever seen in my life. I jumped up and people were looking at me like I was crazy. Once we got to Cancun and were laying on the beach, Sandy asked me if she could go topless. I told her sure. Later that day we called a driver and gentleman by the name of Oscar showed up. I gave him a good tip and he gave me his number and told me to call him anytime we needed to go anywhere. Him and Sandy were talking Spanish and I told them both English only. Don't talk about killing me in Mexico. They both laughed. We went to a restaurant and the line was extremely long. I told Sandy to tell the hostess in Spanish I have a big tip for him. They looked at her and said your reservation is ready, right this way. I gave him a twenty, which I'm not sure how many pesos, but I know it was a lot. He smiled and said thank you and if there was anything that I needed, let him know personally. I ordered the fish and the waiter asked me if I wanted the whole fish. I looked at him and said yes, because I didn't understand. I understood once my meal was brought out. It still had the head on it. I had never eaten fish with the head on it. I took a few bites and was done. I went to a cigar shop, because I wanted to buy my jeweler some Cohiba cigars. Kevino, my jeweler liked cigars and I heard that Cuban Cohibas were the best cigars. I bought a box for $325. I went to another store just to see if I had gotten a good price. I overheard this American guy say that he loved Cohibas, but we couldn't take them back to the US. Anything from Cuba was banned from import into the US. I was pissed because I had just spent my money on them. I called Kevino and told him. He said I could bring a box back with no problem. I was still a little apprehensive, because I was on probation for my gun charge. I was not supposed to leave the state and I was out of the country. Sandy told me she would just put them in her purse when we went through customs. The next morning, I ordered room service. I had some orange juice and it was warm. I grabbed some ice off of the tray and dropped it into my juice. Later that day I began to feel ill on my stomach. Sandy asked what I had ate and I told her. She told me I couldn't use the ice, because we couldn't drink their water. I got so sick I went to the doctor in the hotel. He told me my blood pressure was up. I thought to myself I don't want to die in Mexico. He gave me some medicine and I began to feel better. I called Oscar and told him I needed some homemade chicken noodle soup. He told me we could go and get some, but it was in the barrio. I was like fine and Sandy said no. She explained that barrio meant the hood or ghetto. Sandy grew up in upper class neighborhoods. I told her we would be fine and instructed Oscar to take us to get the soup.

That day gave me new thought on how lucky some of us are, but I also saw that it doesn't take money to be happy. It was nothing but dirt roads and shacks. Kids where everywhere playing soccer and looked happy. I got the soup and sat with locals and ate. They couldn't speak English, so Sandy and Oscar were my translators. I had some good conversations and laughs. Oscar drove me past this house and told me he was the biggest drug dealer in the area. I have no idea why he told me that, but I didn't say a word. I always wondered what would have happened if I tried to get that connect. He told us he wanted to show us his house. It was getting dark and Sandy didn't want to go. I told her it would be disrespectful not to go and besides I could handle Oscar. He pulled up to a little shack. It was made of what looked like tin. There where dirt floors. He was proud of his home and gave me a gift. I accepted the gift thanked him and he gave me a hug. He drove us back to the hotel and told me that he really liked me, and I was a good guy. I didn't understand why, but I just thanked him. Later that night we went on a booze cruise and I made the best of it. The next morning it was time to leave. We go to the airport twenty minutes before our flight was about to leave. They would not allow us to board. I was pissed, because I had a meeting with my probation officer the next day and as I stated, I'm not supposed to be out of the sate let alone the country. I called Oscar and asked him to pick us up at the airport. He told me he couldn't pick us up and we had to catch the bus back to the hotel. We checked back in and he came to the hotel. He explained that the Mexican Mafia controlled all the pickups from the airport. He could drop me off, but he could not pick me up. Sandy was able to find us a flight out the first thing the next morning. We had to stop in Houston for customs. They didn't say anything to Sandy about the cigars. I got back just in time for my meeting with my probation officer. She asked me if I did anything exciting this week. I looked at her and said I was running around Mexico. Then I laughed and said no nothing really this was just a regular old work week. I took Kevino the box of cigars, but he wouldn't accept the box. He took out a couple and told me I should try them. I told him I didn't know the first thing about cigars. He told me to get a humidor to keep them fresh and a lighter and cutter. I was telling him about my trip when Rhonda walked into the store. I had told Kevino I thought she was attractive one day. I went to the restroom and when I returned. I asked Kevino did he want to go and grab something to eat, because he was about to close. He told me had dinner plans. He said to Rhonda, "you said you were hungry, you should go eat with P." Kevino called me P, short for Peanut. Rhonda said no thank you I'm fine. I thought to myself what a bitch. I definitely want to fuck her now. I left and went to this cigar store in Pentagon mall. I bought a $300 lighter and $150 cigar cutter. It was a big fight coming up in Vegas and I wanted to take my pops. I asked my cousin Tank could he go. I told him I was paying for the flight and hotels. All he had to worry about was spending money. He told me he had to check with his wife. I told my partner Pat the same thing. They both agreed. I told Sandy I was taking my pops to Vegas for the fight. She asked, "when are we going and how long are we staying?" She wanted to know how much time to take off. I told her she was not going, and she immediately caught an attitude. The trip was not for three weeks, but we argued about that trip up until the day before I left. She was so worried about what I was going to do on the trip without her. I told her the day before the trip that she didn't need to worry about what I did on the trip because we were no longer together. I wanted to do some shopping before I went to Vegas. I wanted to get some black Versace pants, so me and Tank went to the Versace store in DC. I was looking at some pants when the sale person asked if I was looking for anything particular. I told him what I was looking for. He actually had some black pants in his hand, and I asked could I see those. He said to me that these were expensive. I asked him how much they were, and he said they were $300. I looked at Tank and he just started laughing. I wind up buying some pants that actually cost $600. I pulled out a big wad of cash of about five thousand dollars and the salesperson attitude quickly changed. He gave me his card and asked if I wanted to be put on their mailing list. I declined paid him, left the store and I left his card on the counter. The next morning, we were off to Vegas. My casino Host had a limo pick us up from the airport. The trip started off great. We went to the craps table and I won three thousand in less than an hour. Pat also won the exact same amount and went to play blackjack. He told me he lost a $1,000. The next day we did the exact same thing. I won about three thousand in a short period of time. Pat once again went and lost playing blackjack. We went shopping later that day. I had forgotten to pack a white shirt for one of my suits. I walked into a store and saw they were having a fifty percent off sale on select items. I asked if the shirts were on sale and they said yes. I didn't look at the price and I grabbed two shirts. They rung up the shirts and they came to almost $700. I said I thought they were on sale. The salesperson said they are. I told him to put them back. I was not paying $300 for a plain white shirt. I went in the Hugo boss shop and bought a white shirt for a $150. I also brought a couple Versace suits on sale for $2,000 a piece. Pat is a cool, but an arrogant guy. I told him before we went to Vegas that the money that we have is pennies considered to the type of money that comes through Vegas. That night my casino host had gotten us VIP seating in the hotel club Studio 54. We had ordered a couple bottles of Cristal Champagne. While waiting to be seated, Pat offered some girls a glass of champagne. When our table became available, he asked them to come over to our table and they declined. Me and Tank were laughing so hard. I told him they are probably use to guys giving them bottles not glasses, but don't sweat it. We ran into these girls we had seen earlier from LA. They partied with us. At the end of the night Pat invited them up to his room. Tank said he was going off to do his own thing. Tank and Pat shared a room and me and pops shared a room. We were all laughing and talking when Pat stood in the middle of the floor and began to get naked. I told the girl we should leave. Pat gave me the ten thousand he had on him to hold because he was so drunk. We left and she asked did I want to go and gamble. I told her no let's go to her room. I was also a little tipsy. The next thing I knew we were naked. I asked if she had a condom. She told me we didn't need one because we were not going to do anything. I told her I would be right back. I went and got a condom. I went back and pulled out the condom and asked if she wanted me to leave. She started taking my clothes off. The next thing I knew she was waking me up telling me to get under the covers her girlfriend was coming in the room. I remembered I had Pat's ten and my ten thousand in my jacket. I got up and got dressed and left. Over breakfast we laughed about how drunk Pat was. He talked about how much fun he had with the girl. I told him he probably couldn't remember most of it. We went to play craps that day. While we were playing the girls from LA came up to us and Pat was irritated. I gave them a hundred bucks and told them to go and get some lunch we would catch up with them later after we were done gambling. I told Pat he needed to chill and how much fun he said he had with her the night before. We won again. Pat was about to go and play blackjack. I said to him. For the last three days we have won playing craps, and every day you go and lose playing blackjack. How about you give blackjack a rest today. He agreed and we went to lunch.

That night was the night of the fight and I wanted to bet the fight went past ten rounds. Tank and Pat said Delahoya would knock the dude out before that. We were supposed to have ring side seats. We were in the first row of the first tier. Great seats, but not the ringside seats my host had promised me. I was even more pissed when the fight went to the eleventh round. I would have won seven thousand dollars on my bet had I not listened to them. After the fight I ran into my host. She asked me how the fight was. I told her that the fight was great, but if I was any higher in the stands, I would have bumped my head on the ceiling. She apologized and offered to buy us drinks. We went to the bar and ordered Louie13. She said you guys have expensive taste. I told if she was uncomfortable buying it no worries I would pay for the shots. She laughed and told me don't be ridiculous. We had another round, she put her hand on my thigh and told me if I needed anything else while I was there don't hesitate. Pat said she wanted to fuck me, but I wasn't sure. The next day was our last day. I have no idea why I didn't have any money on me. We were walking past the crap table after lunch. I asked Pat did he have a thousand on him until we got back to the room. He said yeah why? I said this lady is about to shoot the shit out of the ice. We both put a thousand down and twenty minutes later we were both up over ten thousand a piece. She finally crapped out and we had a couple thousand on the table. Not a bad pay for twenty minutes.

As we were packing my pops asked me to give him some money. I think I gave him fifteen hundred or something and he looked at me and said give him some real money. I took all the money I had and threw it on the bed and told him to take whatever he wanted. I never wanted money to be an issue between me and my pops and it never was. When I got back, I went to see Kevino. Rhonda happened to be in the store, and we were talking. I told her I couldn't believe she refused my dinner invitation. She said she didn't and wouldn't refuse a dinner invitation from me. I reminded her of the day Kevino asked her to go to dinner with me. She told me I didn't ask her Kevino did. I laughed and asked her if she wanted to go to dinner. She looked at me, laughed and said of course. She had a tough outer shell, but she was sweet on the inside. We were casually dating, but we began to get close. She told me she wanted to be more than just casual. She said she knew my lifestyle just don't bring disrespect in her face. Pat had told me he wanted to go to New Orleans, and he was going to pay for the flight and hotel since I took care of Vegas. I knew he went to college down there so I thought it was for school or something related. Rhonda told me she was going to the Essence Jazz festival in New Orleans. I told her I was going there as well but had no idea for what. I asked Pat were we going to the Jazz festival and he said yes. A buddy of his whom I didn't know and our connect we had from Chicago was meeting us down there. Pat told me that I needed to buy some sneakers and some shorts because it was going to be too hot in the daytime for suits and slacks. I laughed and said ok. The first day we got there, we were drinking as soon we woke up. We went to a club in the middle of the day and it was packed, and everyone was drinking. I asked the guy how much for one. He said two dollars. I said no How much for one tray full of shots. He said fifty dollars. We began to buy all of his trays and just started giving them out to all the girls. We became the big hit of the party. Needless to say, the girls were all over us. Later that night we rented a limo to go to the Superdome for the Concert. We told the limo driver we would be a couple of hours. We actually came out early and there was no limo. We were pissed to say the least and none of us knew the number to the company. We had to catch a cab back to the hotel. Once we got in touch with the company, I told them they needed to give us a refund. The driver said we said we were going to be a few hours. I explained to them that regardless of how long we say we are staying; we were being charged by the hour and he should be out there waiting. They agreed and told us they would discount us and sent another driver out. We wanted to go to a local club, and we took the driver inside with us. We paid his way and told him if he wanted anything it was on us. Pat ordered eight bottles of Moet champagne and the party was on. We left that club and went to the next club. This club was filled with dudes from DC and Pat ordered ten bottles of Dom Perignon champagne. We were splitting the bill four ways, so it was not that bad. I noticed Pat arguing with this dude, so I walked over to see what was going on. He told me the dude told him to move because he wanted to sit down. I asked Pat had the dude been sitting on the couch you were standing on and he said no. At the same time a group of dudes I knew from DC walked over and asked was I ok. Before I could answer the dude, Pat had been arguing with walked up with two dudes. I pulled the guy to the side and explained we didn't want any trouble. We came to party, but we had no problem tearing this whole place to pieces if they wanted some drama. He looked at the dudes that had walked over to me and agreed. I got a couple of glasses and poured them champagne and told them to have a good night. I reminded Pat that I was on probation and I was not supposed to be out of the state, and he needed to keep my freedom in mind and keep a cool head. He said you know I love you and I got you. I laughed and said shut your drunk ass up and party. We had a blast that night. After the club we went to the river boats to gamble. We both bought in for about three thousand and cashed out seven thousand a piece. When we were cashing our chips in, the cashier asked Pat his name. He said his name was Roy Rogers. I laughed until I got to the window and another cashier asked me the same. I told her Bugsy Siegel. I'm not sure why they asked our name because we didn't win over ten thousand dollars. The next night was pretty much the same. We got a limo and was hoping from party to party. Me and Rhonda ended up at the same club. She told me that she did not want to cramp my style. I laughed and told her that she had nothing to worry about. I brought her a couple bottles of Moet and told her have fun we were leaving to go to another party. We went to this horrible party and was ready to leave. There were about five exotic looking girls from California. I happened to be talking to one and she was talking about how lame the party was. I told her we were leaving the party and they should come with us. She asked how are her girlfriends and my friends going to fit in our car? I told her we had a limo outside that seats twelve. She grabbed her girls and we all jumped in the limo. Pat had some unopened bottles of champagne and we were having a party in the limo. I remember one of the girls taking her top off. That was another fun filled night. The last day they were having a pool party at our hotel. We had made friends with the bar tender in our hotel. We told him we wanted some bottles of Cristal champagne. He could get us a discount, but they still would be expensive. We told him we would take care of him. I remember Ced the entertainer was at the party and some NBA players. One guy from the Wizards who I didn't particular care for because we had a run-in back home with some girls a couple times. The four of us were the only guys actually swimming in the pool. The bartender had hooked us up on the Cristal. He only charged us two hundred dollars a bottle. We bought ten bottles and we gave him a $400 tip. He told us he had something special for us. He had one of the waiters bring us out our champagne on silver platters and serve us in the pool. Everyone was looking like who the fuck are these dudes. We had the pick of any girl in the place. It was like we were celebrities. Rhonda didn't come to the party, but some of her friends must have attended because she told me she heard about us and our shenanigans. I laughed and told her she should have come. I told her she would never be disrespected by me or any female while she was in my company. She thanked me and asked if she could spend the last night with me. I told her of course you can as long as she didn't mind sharing me with this girl from LA. I told her I was joking, because I knew she probably wouldn't but the girl from LA was down with it. I had told the girl from LA my girl was also down here and she asked if she liked girls because she did.

# Chapter 11

# A Hustlers Demise

My last night was a quiet night with Rhonda. Now it was time to go back home and get back to business. When we got back, I called my Columbian and Dominican connects and neither one of them had anything. I had some dudes waiting to buy some keys of coke. This day would change our lives. I went to see my pops and we were sitting and watching tv and I told him of my dilemma. I was going to Vegas that Thursday and didn't have any coke. My pops had an old associate named Donny who had fell off. He was making big money and I believe he started to get high. He had contacted me several times about a Florida connect that he had. I was never interested because I didn't trust Donny, and the prices were generally higher than what I was paying. My pops told me I should give them a try. He said you wouldn't have to go and get it. He was always worried about me going to New York alone. I told him I just didn't know. He told me that he would do the deal if I was nervous about it. I told him absolutely not. I told him I would call Donny. I called Donny and told him that I was leaving town on Thursday and they would have to be here by Tuesday. He called me back and said everything was a go. I had the majority of my money in a safe deposit box. I never went to the box or had a key to the box. I would usually have my sister Ann put money in or take money out. I called Ann and told her I needed a few dollars out of the box. She told me she couldn't go and brought me the key. I put the key on my key ring so I would not lose it. That Tuesday Morning Donny came to my house. He told me the meet was at a hotel not too far from my pops house. I told him I would drop him off at the hotel and for him to catch a cab to my pops house. I was getting four keys at twenty-two thousand a piece. I handed him a bag with eighty-four thousand dollars in it. I told him don't fuck me. I drove him to the hotel and when I pulled away from the hotel. I was pulled over by a Chevy truck with police lights. I immediately knew this was a bust, but I was not worried because I didn't have anything on me. When they took me down to the Fed building the agent said to me. We don't want you we just want who you are taking it too. I immediately knew right then and there they had no clue what was going on. I was not taking it to anyone. I was the man. I knew they had my keys with my safety deposit key on it. I had to think fast. I told them if they get my lawyer down here, I would tell them anything they wanted to know. I told them to call my lawyer Buddy. I wanted to tell Buddy to tell Ann to go to the safety deposit box and get the two hundred thousand dollars I had in it. They told me they couldn't get in touch with Buddy, but they could give me a lawyer. I told them if they could not get in touch with my lawyer I had nothing else to say. They put me and Donny in the car together and he was literally crying like a bitch saying he couldn't go to jail. All I'm thinking is either you go to jail or you snitch on me. Once we got to the jail, Buddy came to see me. He told me my co-defendant was going to tell on me because his court appointed lawyer wanted to come and work in Buddy's office and had given Buddy the heads up. My pops as usual came in and wanted me to fight head on with the feds. He was happy to see me. I was in holding for a day and a half and my family thought someone had kidnapped me and maybe killed me. I was more concerned about what Donny was going to say. The feds had been to the safety deposit box and seized the two hundred thousand dollars. They really had no case against me. I didn't get caught with any drugs, or money at the buy. I never met the guy from Florida who was snitching. The only thing they had was Donny. I was not comfortable with Buddy handling this case. I hired two lawyers Red and Al. They were two of the biggest drug lawyers in the DC area. They came in and told me that most of the government case depended on Donny. Red and Al had already talked to the prosecutor and were trying to work out a deal. They knew that Donny and my pops had done time together. They thought that My pops and Donny had orchestrated the deal. The feds couldn't believe I was the man behind this because they knew nothing about me. I told them my pops had nothing to do with this. They said I had told them I was willing to work with them. I told them I only said that because I was trying to get a lawyer to see me to get a message to my sister. I told them after they couldn't. I told them I had nothing to say. They told me they could use this to my advantage. I told them very clearly that I would not snitch on anyone. Basically, I had no one to snitch on because I was the man. They told me to let them worry about that. They told me they could get me out on bond. I told them fine. They told me their fee was forty thousand and I was like whoa. This is when you find out who really has your back. I called my boy Bo and told him I needed five thousand. He told me to tell him when and where to take the money. I was trying to get in touch with Pat with no success. I got a bond and was back on the street. Me and Pops went to see the lawyers and I kind of understood where the lawyers were coming from. My pops was telling the lawyers that I didn't know Donny he was a friend of his. I told my pops to be quiet before they try to charge him as well. I'm not sure if he was trying to take the charge for me or what he had discussed with the lawyers, I just knew it was not happening. Right before this happened, we had taken a loan out on the house we owned in Maryland for a hundred thousand. I was against it, because I had the money to pay off the stuff pops wanted to pay off. It was always difficult for me to tell my pops no. We had paid off somethings and had forty thousand sitting in the bank. The government seized the money and told me that if we didn't forfeit the money, they would seize the house. They said they had someone who was going to say they bought drugs from me at the house. I told my lawyers that was a lie and impossible. They said in a civil case all they have to do is put a person on the stand. They asked me did I know a girl named Jaime and I replied no. They asked me did I know BB. Jaime was BB's wife and now I put it together. They said Jaime and BB told the Feds if they needed any evidence against me, they could supply it. I knew BB had snitched on Black and probably was going to set me up back in the day. I told the lawyers I would make a deal with the government and give them twenty thousand of the forty thousand. I had to pay that money back with interest. Theses lawyers were really working both sides of the fence. They had allowed the feds to confiscate my truck when Sunny went to make a payment before I got a bond. They told me that the prosecutors knew I was not going to snitch on my pops and I once again told them he had nothing to do with this. They wanted to paint a picture of me being on drugs, they knew about my moms and my pops being in jail. The story they wanted to paint was I was just giving a ride to a friend of my pops in hopes that I might get some drugs, but in no way was I some type of major player. It's crazy how things work. When I had my gun charge. They made me take a urine and I tested positive for cocaine. Now I have never ever tried cocaine in my life, but the touching and cooking of it I guess it had gotten into my system. They were going to use that to say I was on drugs and needed help. They also wanted to throw in account that I would be surely violated with my current probation. I'm not sure what kind of deals they were working on behind the scenes, while I was on bond. I had called my connect Dre. Dre already knew I had been locked up. I told him I needed some money to pay for my lawyer. He told me shit was tight and had I talked to Pat. He told me Pat told him that I might be telling. I told him if I was Hot you and Pat would be in jail right now. He agreed, but still told me money was tight. I finally caught up to Pat and he gave me a couple thousand. I saw another dude and he told me Pat had said I might be telling as well. I called Pat and said we needed to talk immediately. I asked him about this, and he said he was asked if he thought I would tell, and he said he didn't know. I was furious with Pat. I told him if I was telling you would be the first one gone. You were basically my righthand man. Second, I came to your defense when you saw the dude that shot you. Third, I came to your defense when word was out that you might be snitching. What he didn't know. It was some dudes that wanted to kill him because they thought he was snitching before my situation and thought he might have snitched on me. I stopped anything from happening to him in both scenarios. I also had another issue right before I got locked up. I had went into business with this dude I knew name Tre. His pops had a trash company and he had a dump truck. He came to me and asked if I wanted to go into business with him. He explained the dump truck business and how it could be profitable. I looked at it as a way to clean up my money. I gave him fifteen thousand dollars to lease a new dump truck. He came to me for another fifteen for another truck. I told him that was it. When I got locked up. I asked if the trucks were making money and we got into a heated argument. Needless to say. I was about to go to his house and Sunny talked me out of it. She told me I was out on bond and could not afford to get into any more trouble. After I calmed down, I agreed. This dude fucked me out of thirty thousand and then became a cop. My lawyers worked out a deal for me to forfeit the two hundred thousand dollars, twenty thousand from the bank and my truck that was paid for that was worth at least thirty-five thousand. They also had confiscated the eighty-four thousand dollars from Donny. I didn't snitch on anyone and that can be fact checked. My name was never in any one's paperwork point blank period. The deal was I would be violated by the judge in my gun case and have to do three years. After that I would come home and have to do five years of Supervised probation. The feds are so dirty. The order was for four keys of cocaine. They threw in an extra key of cocaine to try to change the statue. See if you get caught with four keys or less of cocaine and never been in any trouble you can get anywhere from probation to five years. The judge was actually upset with the agents because this was basically a violation of the law. One thing I learned about federal judges is that that they follow the law and don't like for it to be circumvented. During times of trouble you really find out who cares for you. Although me and Sunny had went our separate ways she stood up for me. Although me and Rhonda had become very close. When everything started happening. I told her it would be best for her to move on, because I had no idea what type of time I was facing. I felt it would be unfair for me to ask her to make that type of sacrifice in our short relationship. I was given a date to turn myself in. I had so many emotions going on through those weeks leading up to the time I was going in. I was happy, mad and frustrated. My goal was to get five hundred thousand dollars and get out of the game. I was at three hundred thousand. I had plans on buying a trash company for two hundred fifty thousand dollars and have the other two fifty for a safety blanket. My goal was in sight. I was going to achieve that goal in another six months if everything went as plan. As you can see it did not. I was happy that I stood tall like my pops had always told me to do. I didn't snitch on anyone and no one else was hurt by what I had done directly. Yes, my family was hurt that I had to go away to prison, but it was what we had become accustomed to. I was fortunate the feds jumped the gun and didn't just allow Donnie to deliver the drugs and then put me under surveillance. It would have been a big conspiracy case and I'm sure I would have been at the top and might still be in Jail. I remember while I was on bond Tank came and said to me look at the bright side. At the time I didn't understand what he was talking about. Once I went inside, I started to realize what he was talking about. I had people wanting to kidnap and kill me for my money. I never cared because I was always strapped. I also knew when people couldn't get you, they would try to kidnap someone you love and hold them for ransom. I remember telling my pops to stay home sometime, because I never wanted anything to happen to him. He was just like me and said fuck them and ain't nothing going to happen to him, and he was not going to stop living his life. I turned myself in and started to do my time. I had been locked up before on the gun charge. I knew the routine and what to expect. When you go to jail you just carry yourself like a man. You mind your business and don't take no shit if it comes your way. I was almost a year in jail and I was pissed because I was still being held in the DC area. I wanted to get shipped out of the DC area to a federal facility, because the DC jail was bullshit. They told me since I had an appeal that was in process. They would not ship me out until my appeal had been ruled on. In jail I read a lot and played chess. I was grateful that I was close, and my family could come and visit me.

During that whole year my mom never came to see me once. She never came to see me when I was locked up for the couple months when I had the gun charge either. I never knew or asked why, but it did hurt my feelings. Sunny was not coming regular either, but my pops and Ann always came to see me. I wouldn't allow our son to come and see me. I told Sunny to tell him I was away on business. I'm not sure if Sunny ever told him the truth. I never wanted him to see the inside of a prison like I did growing up. One day when I called home. Sunny told me that Bobby my lawyer from my gun case wanted me to give him a call and that it was important. I gave him a call and he asked me if I was ready to come home. I told him stop playing I had three years to do. He told me that the appeals court had reversed my gun charge and that prosecution was not going to retry the case so I would be free very soon. I was shocked and so excited. I had my mind set to do another two years and now I was about to be free. Sunny had went back to work before I came in. I had told her when I come home that I was not going back to selling drugs, but I was going back into the business with the girls and just make it an escort service. If she wasn't cool with that to let me know. She said she was fine with it as long as she could be my number one. I agreed as long as she took care of my business. I have to say when I got out it was a feeling of true liberation. It was hilarious to me that as soon as I got out. All the dudes I use to supply were trying to get in touch with me to see if I was back hustling. I told them all that I was done with that life. I had gotten jammed up and got lucky so to speak. None of them really stood with me except Bo and D Rock. D Rock and Pat were cousins. I had been dealing with D Rock for a couple years and he was always a solid guy. When I came home D Rock asked me if I needed anything and don't hesitate if I did. Once I was home. I got a new car and went to work. Me and Tank set out on a mission to get me girls to work. Once I was home me and Sunny where not in a good place. She was back drinking and we just were not getting along. I had an apartment where the girls worked out of and still had my house in Maryland. Sunny stopped coming home and staying at the apartment. She said it was so she could get more money, but I knew something else was up. I wind up coming up with a girl from West Virginia. She was making about twelve to fifteen hundred a day. Sunny didn't like it. She ran her away and then she told me she was unhappy and leaving. I was pissed, but not surprised. Some people can love you so much that somehow, they become to hate you and want to destroy you. I think in her mind since she couldn't have kids, she felt like she would never be enough for me. She really was at the point where she didn't want me to have other girls besides her. I wished her the best, and told her if it was anything, I could do to help her I would. So now I was in a weird place I had not been in before. No source of income. I was on federal probation and my probation officer was cool. The crazy thing was her supervisor had been my pops probation officer. My pops told me he used to give her weed and he had fucked her. When I told my probation officer Sunny was no longer with me. She told me if I ever needed to talk, I could always call her. I was not about to get involved with my probation officer.

Times were a little difficult and I decided to sell my house. I moved in with my pops in his house in DC. My probation officer told me one day that although she like me, she was not going to lose her job because of me. Meaning I had to get a job. Tank was working at a big law firm in downtown DC. He was a supervisor of the company that handled all of their professional stuff such as copying, faxing, emailing and the mail system among other things for the firm. He got me a job there. His now wife was my direct supervisor. After about six months on the job I had gotten a promotion. People were upset that I had got the promotion. I had worked on a floor were only the partners of the firm worked. The guy who ran that floor was quitting. My supervisor went to the secretaries of all the partners and asked whom they would like to fill the vacant position. They unanimously picked me. I had recently come up with a girl and she was doing about twelve hundred to two thousand a day. My supervisor told me if I took the position I could not quit. I told her I needed the job for probation purposes. A few months later I was in a predicament where I was forced to choose between my job and my business. I was only making about fourteen hundred every two weeks opposed to fourteen hundred a day. I apologized to my supervisor, but I chose my business. Tank was able to duplicate old pay stubs to give to my probation officer. This went on for the next couple years traveling all over the country. My pops would be pissed with me because I was not supposed to be out of the state, but I was all over the country. I remember one time I had been out of town for about two weeks. When I got back, I told my pops I needed for him to put some money in the bank. All the way to the bank he was telling me how I have to stop going out of town. If I get caught out of town I'm going back to jail. When we got to the bank. I handed him eighteen thousand dollars. He said you made all that in two weeks. I told him I actually made more, but I had to pay for expenses and shopping trips. He smiled and then he said your ass still need to stop going out of town. On my next trip out of town. He called me one day and told me it was mandatory I come home. He told me he was selling his house. I tried to talk him out of it, but his mind was made up. I think deep down he felt responsible for me dealing with Donny and wanted to give me a new start. I started to go to real estate school. After I finished school. I called two realtors to list the property. I told them we wanted four hundred and fifty thousand dollars for the house. The first realtor told me he could probably get me four twenty-five. The second one told me about the same thing. I listed the house and sold it for four hundred and fifty-one thousand dollars and didn't have to pay the six percent commission.

Me and pops moved in together and I started to invest in the Baltimore real estate market. That December my pops went into the hospital. He had been in the hospital a few years prior and it looked like he wasn't going to make it. He pulled through like a champ and was better than ever. This time I thought the same thing that he would pull through again. On January 3rd the day he was born, eighty-four years later would be the day that he would die. I remember waking up that morning saying I was going to skip my appraisal class and spend his birthday with him. I got a call from my uncle telling me to get to the hospital as soon as possible. When I got there two of my sisters where there. The doctor told us my pops was really weak and probably was not going to make it. Later that day he passed away. I was totally crushed and felt so alone. I immediately thought about the last time I had told him I loved him. It had been a while. I didn't grow up in a household that expressed affection. I was talking to Tank who had loss his dad. I told him I had never told my pops I loved him as an adult. He told me I should because he never got to tell his pops he loved him as an adult. I remember being at the gambling house a few years prior and it was just me and pops. It took me about thirty minutes of just sitting there to say hey pops, I love you. He looked at me kind of funny and asked me was everything ok. I said yes, I just wanted to tell you I love you. He smiled and said I love you too, but we know we love each other by how we treat and respect each other. Then he challenged me to a card game. No matter what happened or went on in my life my pops was always my rock. I remember him asking me at breakfast a few months prior. What am I going to do when he dies? He was eighty-three at the time, but he seemed to be in great health for a man his age. He did everything for himself. He was still driving, cooking and even sexually active.

That first week was the hardest. Every night I went out and got drunk, until one day I looked in the mirror and knew my pops would be pissed with me. He didn't like me to drink at all let alone get drunk. I started to concentrate on my real estate business, but the market crashed and I loss every dime. I was in a really dark place. See times like this I always had my pops to lean on. He would say something like, "No sense in you looking like that, you know what to do go get some money."

I didn't want to deal with girls anymore and I definitely was not going to sell drugs again. I remember every Sunday if I was in town me and my pops would watch the Sopranos and the Wire. I always saw him if I was in town, but those Sunday's were special. I later started and continued that same Sunday tradition with my mom until her death. I called Tank and he got me a job at a new law firm he was working at. I was quickly promoted again. I had started to work out and change my nutrition before my pops had died. He had diabetes and I was started to gain a lot of weight. I knew it was a good possibility if I didn't make some changes, I could also get the disease. I had people asking me all the time if I was a trainer when I would work out in the gym. One particular gym I use to work out at, one of the trainers asked me if I had ever thought about being a trainer. He told me a good trainer could make six figures. One day I decided to do some research and ordered a training program. I got certified. I walked into a gym one day and asked to speak with their personal training manager. When he walked out. He asked if he could help me. I looked him dead in the eye and said I'm one of your new trainers. He smiled and said let's talk. About an hour later he offered me the job. I started training and loved it. I later went on to get certified as a Life Coach. The two certifications helped me to help thousands to get in the best shapes of their lives mentally and physically. I took some time off and got my Commercial Driver's License as well. I also traveled the country playing poker. I would tell some of my stories at poker games, and I would always hear the same thing. You should write a book. SO I DID!!!!

As I look back over my life it was filled with gifts and curses. As a child I was gifted with everything money could buy, but I was cursed with losing my pops from the age 12 to 16 on a daily basis. I was gifted to have him return and save my life when I was 16 only to lose my mom. I had any woman of my choice but could never find the one to give me the child I wanted. I was at the top of my game in two different games and it all came to an end. Today I'm gifted to be happy and helping others to find happiness. No curses. Today my life is absolutely amazing.

I dedicate this book to my Pops, mom and sister who passed away

CPSIA information can be obtained
at www.ICGtesting.com
Printed in the USA
FSHW020725010420
68695FS

9 780578 665153